TENNIS:
Teaching, Coaching, and Directing Programs

TENNIS:
Teaching, Coaching, and Directing Programs

Jim Brown

McNeese State University

PRENTICE-HALL, Inc.   Englewood Cliffs, New Jersey

Library of Congress Cataloging in Publication Data

BROWN, JIM, 1940–
    Tennis: teaching, coaching, and directing
programs.

Bibliography: p.
Includes index.
    1. Tennis.   I. Title.
GV995.B6927   796.34′22   75-33047
ISBN 0-13-903344-0

Printed in the United States of America

10   9   8   7   6   5   4   3   2

PRENTICE-HALL INTERNATIONAL, INC., *London*
PRENTICE-HALL OF AUSTRALIA PTY. LIMITED, *Sydney*
PRENTICE-HALL OF CANADA, LTD., *Toronto*
PRENTICE-HALL OF INDIA PRIVATE LIMITED, *New Delhi*
PRENTICE-HALL OF JAPAN, INC., *Tokyo*
PRENTICE-HALL OF SOUTH-EAST ASIA PRIVATE LIMITED, *Singapore*

Contents

3

TEACHING THE GAME   53

4

COACHING THE SPORT   83

5

DIRECTING PROGRAMS   115

6

DRILLS   151

Preface

This is a book for those who already know something about tennis. You will not find the traditional sections on tennis history, a glossary of terms, instructions for the Western grip, or comments on tennis etiquette. What you will find are practical suggestions to help teachers, coaches, and others who supervise tennis programs. Knowing how to play the game is merely the first step toward becoming a successful tennis administrator. It is assumed that you know how to play. Here is information on how to transmit that knowledge to others and to design programs so that others may benefit from your expertise.

The first section describes some of the common flaws players develop in their strokes and tells you how those players might correct the flaws. If you can learn to observe what a player does correctly or incorrectly, you will be at least a step ahead of the majority of your peers.

The second section contains information on how to make tennis knowledge and skill work for a player in a match situation. Good strokes are not enough. They must be used at the right time, on the right court, and against the right player to be effective.

If there is any theory in this book, it is contained in the first half of "Teaching the Game." Many teachers get into tennis instruction without a background in psychology, communications skills, or human growth and development. Reading a few chapters on these subjects will not qualify a person in those areas, but it may stimulate the reader to look at his or her methods of getting along with the people being taught. The second half of the section reverts to practical teaching material.

Coaching tennis involves more than teaching people how to play the game. The tennis teacher is a purist. The tennis coach is a teacher, public relations director, promoter, organizer, and mediator. Perhaps you can better fulfill all of those roles if you read about what other coaches have found to be successful techniques.

There is a large group of tennis administrators who work as club pros, directors of municipal programs, camp counselors, and YMCA-YWCA instructors. They work with a more diverse group of players than teachers and coaches. If their players are to enjoy tennis, effective organization of large groups is necessary. The fifth section of the book is designed to give information to the program directors.

The last section contains diagrams and descriptions of tennis drills. Regardless of your specific job, sooner or later you will have to show or tell people how to use their practice time efficiently. The drills shown in the last chapters involve practice routines for all aspects of the game.

I would like to thank the tennis players of Lake Charles, Louisiana, for their help in making this book possible. Burl Vincent and the people who posed for pictures were especially helpful. Photographs are by Burl Vincent and Jim Brown.

TENNIS:
Teaching, Coaching, and
Directing Programs

1 *Recognizing Flaws in Strokes*

RECOGNIZING FLAWS IN STROKES

If there is one ability of a tennis teacher or coach that will help you earn the respect of those being taught, it is probably the ability to observe what a player is doing wrong and to make a correction that solves the problem. A player will have confidence in someone who can suggest a change that brings immediate, observable results.

The ability to give technical assistance is not limited to those who were or are outstanding players. It is a skill that can be learned by conscientious students of tennis. Some people know how to play the game, but have not had the time or interest to learn how to teach it. Others are still so wrapped up in their own games that they cannot concentrate on learning to teach or coach.

A factor which further supports the theory that mediocre players can be excellent tennis instructors is the fact that every tennis player makes the same kinds of errors. For example, it would not be unusual for a world class player to develop a problem with the serve because of an incorrect toss. A poor toss can also create problems for college players, high school players, and the eight-year-old taking his* first lesson. It does not take a tennis genius to learn where the ball should be tossed prior to a serve. Once that is learned, it is easy to watch a player and to determine if the ball is being tossed properly.

Some teachers and coaches are awed or intimidated by those who know more technical tennis than they do. Professional respect is admirable, but you should not feel that you have nothing to offer your students or players just because there are people who can offer more. No one acquires a great depth of technical knowledge overnight. Knowing how

*Masculine pronouns are used throughout this book to simplify technical descriptions and should be construed to designate both sexes.

to teach fundamentals, how to spot flaws in strokes, and how to make corrections is learned slowly, in small doses, year after year. These skills are acquired by playing the game yourself, by observing other players, by talking to players, teachers, and coaches, by reading books and magazine articles, and occasionally figuring out something by yourself. Every good teacher had to start by learning one little bit of information. If you have not begun the process, now is a good time to start.

If you decide to try to give some technical advice to your players, do not overcoach. Try to spot one problem area in each player and make a suggestion to correct that particular problem. If a player is successful with a stroke, let it and him alone, even if the stroke is a bit unorthodox. Finally, do not be afraid to say "I don't know," if a player asks for help on a stroke and you cannot give it immediately. With more time and experience, perhaps both of you working together can find the solution to a stroke problem. In this chapter, the term stroke is a general one that includes all the components of a shot, not just the swing itself.

THE SERVE

The first problem area for the serve may be the position of the feet. How are they aligned in relation to the baseline—straight ahead, at a forty-five degree angle, or with the outside of the foot parallel to the line? In most cases, the forty-five degree angle stance is preferable. One exception might be for the flatter serve, in which the feet may be placed in a more straight-ahead position. On a severe topspin serve, some players might stand at a ninety-degree angle to the baseline. In any case, whenever your player is having trouble with the direction of the serve, check the starting position.

The feet are important throughout the serve. What does the server do with them once the service motion starts? Are they together? Apart? How far apart? The feet should be spread far enough to enable the server to shift his weight forward without losing balance. There are two methods of bringing the back foot forward as the serve is delivered. First, the server can bring the back foot all the way from the rear to a position inside the court as the ball is hit. This is done in one motion. The back foot is used to push the body forward as the service motion begins and to restore balance after the ball is hit.

In the second method, the server brings the back foot forward and even with the left foot (if the server is righthanded) just before the moment of impact with the ball. This movement results in a springboard effect into the service motion and may even give the player added height and leverage if he goes up on his toes as he hits. After the ball has been served, the foot continues forward, again for balance or as the first step in moving toward a volleying position.

Both methods of service footwork are acceptable. Watch the top ten players in the world and you will see both styles. The important thing to know is what your player is doing. If he has a timing problem or if there does not seem to be a rhythmic pattern to the service motion, suggest that he try both footwork methods, then decide which is better. Shorter players tend to use the two-step approach.

Next, check your player's toss. It should be slightly in front of the body, slightly beyond the imaginary plane of the baseline, and as high as the server can reach with the arm and racket extended. Unless the player is attempting some kind of unusual topspin or slice serve, the toss should always be made to that same spot. The ball is either there, or the toss is bad. The player in Figure 1-1 has not tossed the ball in front of the body. As a result, he must lean back to make contact with the ball instead of leaning forward, which would allow him to move his body's weight into the service motion. The player in Figure 1-2 has tossed the ball too far to his right, forcing him to lose the forward momentum of the service motion and to be off balance as he hits the ball.

When the toss is properly executed, the swing almost has to be correct in order to make contact with the ball. When the toss is somewhere else—high, low, wide, or inside—the serve has little chance of going in. When you observe the player's toss in practice, stand in several positions near the server. A point directly behind the server enables you to determine whether the ball is going up wide to either side. A position to the side of the server permits you to tell whether the ball is being tossed in front of the body rather than directly above or behind the server's head.

There is one other flaw that is easy to spot. Watch for the player who thinks he has to toss the ball a mile high in order to get enough momentum to hit the ball with force. Encourage your players to toss just high enough for the ball to reach its peak at the point of the arm and racket extension. At that height, the service motion will be continuous, smooth, rhythmic, and have less margin of error than with the higher toss.

The service motion is very similar to throwing a baseball in an overhanded motion. This is the starting point. When working with young high school players, check out their throwing motions before letting them serve. If they cannot throw, they cannot serve.

Every player will have a slightly different serving motion. Since it is impractical if not impossible to teach everyone exactly the same

Figure 1-1. Service toss too far to the rear.

motion, do not try. Just see that both hands drop at the same time, rise at the same time, that the server is not stiff-armed during the motion, and that the ball is hit when the arm is extended. If something is wrong with the swing, the flaw should be spotted in one of these elements of the motion.

Now you can observe the feet, the toss, and the swing with some degree of knowledge. What if the ball still does not go where it is supposed to go? There could be a hundred reasons, so do not consider yourself a failure if you do not know the answer. You may have to go back and check the grip. It should be almost like the backhand grip.

The problem could be a lack of concentration instead of some technical flaw. If the serve is consistently just out or hitting the tape, the problem probably is technical and can be spotted and corrected. If the player is serving into the bottom of the net or out by several feet, he has

Figure 1-2. Service toss too far to the right side.

his mind somewhere other than the tennis court. There is no sure answer for this problem. For some players, a kick in the trunks might work best. For others, a target on the court, a reward, a nickel bet, a look straight into their eyes, or a word of encouragement might work better.[1]

THE FOREHAND

It is impossible to isolate the forehand stroke from the preparation for the stroke, so always consider the possibility that the problem, if there is one, involves getting ready to hit rather than hitting. Watch your player without watching the ball for a while. Is he getting to the ball just in time to hit or is he getting there early, setting up, and then hitting? He should be getting there early. If not, he leaves no time to

[1] Jim Brown, "Flaw Finish: #1, The Service," *Scholastic Coach*, 43, no. 9 (May 1974), 44.

make late, split-second adjustments to direction, pace, spin, or bad bounces.

Second, how are the feet and shoulders positioned as part of the preparation? On most shots the feet and shoulders should be in a position similar to the stance one takes in hitting a baseball. The feet should be spread to a distance slightly wider than the shoulders and the feet should be positioned in a closed stance. In tennis, a closed stance is one in which the feet are pointing toward the sideline and parallel to it. This position allows the weight to be transferred forward as the ball is hit. Power and depth result from this forward weight transfer. Without it, the most beautiful stroke in the world will probably be weak and become weaker as the match progresses. The player in Figure 1-3 has not brought her left foot around to a position so that both feet would form a line parallel to the sideline.

Finally, what is happening with the racket during the preparation for the forehand stroke? The racket should be brought back either parallel to the ground or slightly lower, and the backswing should be executed before the ball bounces on the court prior to the shot. In Figure 1-4, the ball has already bounced and begun to rise, but the player's racket is still in front of her body. Some teachers and coaches tell their players to begin the backswing as soon as they see the ball leave their opponent's racket. Again, the sooner the racket is brought back, the more time the player has to concentrate on hitting and making last-second adjustments, if they are necessary.

Figure 1-3. Open stance preparation for a forehand.

Figure 1-4. Inadequate (late) preparation for a forehand.

So much for the preparation; now look at the swing itself. One of the most common faults is the big windup, big swing (see Figure 1-5). The player who uses the big motion is probably not getting the forward weight transfer mentioned earlier. The backswing should be short enough so that the opponent cannot see the racket at the back of the backswing. The player who uses an excessive backswing creates his own energy crisis, increases the margin of error for the upcoming shot, and has trouble adjusting to faster courts. While he takes the exaggerated backswing, the ball slides by.

The second trouble spot is the trajectory of the racket as it moves forward on the forehand stroke. This motion can result in problems such as chipping, slicing, and excessive topspin. If there is a problem, check to see if the racket is moving slightly upward as it goes forward. The upward and forward trajectory of the racket will eliminate chopping the ball and impart a bit of topspin to the ball, which is exactly what you and your player should want. Although there are occasions when a player might hit a shot with backspin from the baseline area (for example, on some service returns), in most cases the downward racket motion on the forehand is used when the ball is shoulder high or above and will be hit from a position inside the baseline. In those situations, the idea is to crunch downward on the ball for a down-the-line winner or strong approach shot.

The third and perhaps most common flaw in the forehand stroke is the floppy wrist. Sometimes emphasizing a stiff wrist in groundstrokes

Figure 1-5. Excessive backswing preparation for a forehand.

leads to a stiff everything else, but the object is to make the wrist a somewhat inflexible extension of the forearm. If a player is too "wristy," the result is wildness and inconsistency. You may need two sets of guidelines regarding the wrist. The average player will have to play it by the book, keeping the wrist relatively fixed for the sake of control. However, if you are lucky enough to have advanced players, do not be too quick to discourage the selective use of the quick wrist on forehands. If that violates what you have been taught, just watch Laver, Newcombe, or Okker hit the forehand.

Also examine the point of contact between the racket and the ball. Just as in baseball, if a righthanded player is hitting the ball too far in front of the body, he will pull the ball to the left. If contact is made too late, the ball will slide off to the right. On the forehand, most teachers will instruct their players to strike the ball just as it reaches a point even with the body. Some coaches advise their players to make contact slightly in front of the body. As a matter of fact, every player probably makes contact with the ball at a range of points within reach of the racket, but problems develop when the ball is hit much too soon or much too late. The player in Figure 1-6 is making contact with the ball too late.

There are many other possible flaws in this or any other stroke, but the last one to be discussed here will be the follow through. The young player will tend not to follow through at all, resulting in a jabbing motion. Stopping the swing of the racket too soon or following through in

Figure 1-6. Late contact with the ball on a forehand.

the wrong direction can cause wildness as easily as the other problems mentioned. Check to see if your problem player is following through upward across the chest and outward toward the net. He must carry the ball on the strings, and the motion after the hit should be smooth, continuous, and sweeping. This motion is easy to see and easy to practice, even without an opponent. The player can stand in front of a mirror and practice the follow through, analyzing his own stroke.

Remember to look for one thing at a time. Watch to see what your player is doing before the ball gets to his side of the net. If he passes that test, visually measure the size of the swing. Allow room for individuality, but not for a windmill swing. If your player is two for two, watch for the upward motion of the swing, and look to see where contact with the ball is made. If everything is still okay, the wrist will probably also pass. Finally, watch the racket after the hit instead of looking at the ball. If you still cannot spot a flaw, leave that player alone and move on to someone who needs help.[2]

THE BACKHAND

Before considering some of the flaws in the backhand stroke, try to dismiss the misconception that the backhand is a more natural motion

[2]Jim Brown, "Flaw Finish: #2, The Forehand," *Scholastic Coach*, 44, no. 6 (February 1975) 28.

than the forehand, and that the backhand should be easier to learn and execute. Some tennis teachers like to use this argument, perhaps because they heard it somewhere and it sounded good, or perhaps because they are trying to "con" their players. However, there is little evidence to support the natural backhand argument. There are practically no examples of the across-the-body motion in other sports. Arm movement in other sports more closely parallels the forehand swing (throwing, reaching, pulling, pushing, etc.). On the contrary, there is massive evidence that the backhand is a more difficult shot to learn. A quick survey of the number of players having trouble with the grip, stance, and swing is convincing.

Here are some ways to spot some of the common problems in the backhand stroke and to correct them. First, make sure that the player is using the nonracket hand on the racket throat between shots. After every shot he should bring the racket back to a center-of-the-body position with one hand on the grip and one on the throat. The hand on the throat should be there to facilitate the change to the backhand grip if two grips are used, and to guide the racket back on the backswing. While the hand is there, it can also give a push to begin the forward racket motion. In Figure 1-7, the player is not using the nonracket hand on the backswing.

Second, watch to see when the racket goes into the backswing position. Just as in the forehand, the racket should be brought back as early as possible. Many players get into trouble because they wait too long to prepare for the shot. If something goes wrong, there is not time to adjust. The flaw that surfaces will be shots that are sliced off to a

Figure 1-7. Not using the non-racket hand in preparing to hit a backhand.

righthander's left side of the court. The correction may be to begin the backswing sooner.

The ball will also shoot off to the left side because of another problem—making contact too late (Figure 1-8). It is essential that the inexperienced high school or college level player make contact with the ball well in front of the body. Striking the ball even with or behind the body not only telegraphs where the shot will go, but also puts more strain on the arm, resulting in a lack of power. To spot this potential flaw, position yourself to the side of the court even with the player being observed. Watch only your player; concentrate on the point of contact; and you should be able to determine where the ball is being hit in relation to the position of the body. Advanced players may alter the pattern somewhat, but at most levels of play, routine backhand groundstrokes will be hit in front of the body.

Figure 1-8. Late contact with the ball on a backhand.

Another common backhand flaw is the position of the elbow both on the backswing and the stroke itself. On the backswing, the elbow should be tucked in close to the body's midsection. As the forward motion begins, the arm may extend some, but not very much. Do not let your players hit with an extended, stiff armed delivery, and do not let them lead the stroke with the elbow. The motion revolves around the shoulder, not the elbow or wrist. If the elbow is kept relatively close to the body, the shot should be crisp and the restricted motion will reduce the margin of error.

One of the worst things that can happen on the backhand is the "peek-a-boo" elbow. It is not uncommon to see players peering out over their elbows as the backhand stroke begins (Figure 1-9). This uplifted elbow can only result in balls going somewhere other than in, so try to make your players drop their sights (elbows). The best places to observe this flaw are directly in front of the hitter or even with the hitter on the backhand side.

Lifting the shoulder of the arm used to hit the backhand shot can also cause problems. On all groundstrokes, the shoulder closest to the net should be kept down. If not, the player (as the player in Figure 1-10) may fall away from the ball, losing power, instead of moving the weight of the body into the ball.

Finally, the follow through should be carried out in the direction of the shot, then up and across the front of the body. Tell your players to think of carrying the ball on the strings as long as possible, or to think of touching the net with the backs of their hands, or to think of slapping their opponents with the backs of their hands, or to reach out with the racket before bringing it across the body.

Here is a quick review. Remember to look for only one thing at a time and not to try to revamp someone's entire stroke in one practice session. (1) Where is the player's nonracket hand? It should be a second racket hand, especially on the backhand. Connors, Evert, Drysdale, Borg, and others made the two handed backhand a permanent part of the game. (2) When does your player bring the racket back to prepare for the backhand? The sooner the better. (3) Where is the elbow? It should be relatively close to the body on the forward motion and closer

Figure 1-9. "Peek-a-boo" elbow—holding the elbow too high in preparing to hit a backhand.

Figure 1-10. Lifting the shoulder while hitting a backhand.

than that on the backswing. The racket head leads the stroke, not the elbow. (4) Where is contact made with the ball? If slicing is the problem, hitting the ball sooner may be the answer. Keeping the shoulder down will also help the player to avoid the slice. (5) What is happening on the follow through? Remember that the arm and racket go out, up, and across, in that order.[3]

THE VOLLEY

A tennis coach or teacher can be more successful at recognizing flaws in the volley and making the necessary corrections than in any other stroke. There is less time to think about hitting shots at the net, the stroke is much more compact, and there is less room for variations in style. All of these factors make the stroke relatively easy to teach, at least from a mechanical point of view. The fewer the components, the simpler the mechanics, and the easier it should be to spot problems when they develop.

As with most strokes in tennis, one of the first problems might be in preparing for the shot. First, make sure that the player at the net is not trying to change from a forehand to a backhand grip with each shot. There is simply no time to make a change at the net, so the grip should be a Continental, and the racket should be carried high and pointing

[3]Jim Brown, "Flaw Finish: #3, The Backhand," *Scholastic Coach*, 44, no. 7 (March 1975) 8.

directly at the opponent while the volleyer is in the ready position. The player in Figure 1-11 is hitting a backhand volley with a forehand grip rather than with a Continental grip.

Second, watch the backswing to make sure that the racket does not go too far back (see Figure 1-12). Stand to the side of the player and on a line even with his back. As the backswing is taken, you should not be able to see the racket break the plane formed by the person's back. At least try this technique as a corrective measure. In reality, the racket may come back far enough to break the plane, but if the backswing is obviously too big, suggest a more compact approach to the shot. If the problem persists, try standing the player with his back touching the fence surrounding the court. Have someone toss or hit balls to him so that they can be returned with a volley. With his back to the wall, the volleyer will have to shorten the swing or bump the fence with the racket.

Another flaw easily spotted from the side of the court involves the player letting the ball play him instead of going out and getting the ball while it is in front of the body. The secret is to teach your players to attempt to pivot forward into the shot as the ball approaches. For the righthander, that means stepping forward with the left foot for the forehand volley and with the right foot on the backhand side. The other foot is used to make the pivoting movement. Many players, even those at the intermediate and advanced levels, either wait for the ball and make

Figure 1-11. Hitting a backhand volley with a forehand grip instead of a Continental grip.

Figure 1-12. Excessive backswing preparation for a forehand volley.

no pivot, or execute a reverse pivot away from the ball. Either error can result in a powerless volley. The player in Figure 1-13 has let the ball get too far past him instead of making contact while the ball is approaching his position. One method of teaching your players to meet the ball in front of the body is to have a two-on-one rapid fire volley drill. The coach can stand close to the volleyer at one side to observe if the pivot is being made and to verbally remind the player when he forgets to pivot.

The third possible flaw is the actual swinging motion. In the volley, the action takes place at the elbow joint. The volley is punched, not swung at, stroked, or anything else. Since the movement is primarily from the elbow, it is important that the wrist stays firmly in place. The volleyer cannot afford to have a loose, floppy wrist at the net or anywhere else. If the wrist is held firmly in place and the player uses a Continental grip, the racket head will always be held higher than the wrist. The angle of the racket to the forearm is almost ninety degrees. Even on low shots, the grip, wrist, and racket angle stay the same. The player just has to bend his knees to get down on eye level with the ball. Not getting down may even be a flaw itself. Some players like to stand straight up and "golf" at low volleys. It does not work.

The next possible problem to watch for is the player who constantly has to reach too far for the ball (Figure 1-14). The farther the reach, the less the power and accuracy of the volleyer. Emphasize to your players that they must get close to the ball when hitting a volley. If the

Figure 1-13. Late contact with the ball on a forehand volley.

pivot·is made properly, this problem may not exist. To check a player, have him go through the two-on-one drill mentioned earlier, but stand behind him to get a better look at how far away from the ball he is when it is hit.

The last checkpoint is the follow through. As in the backhand, the ball should be carried on the strings as long as possible. Many inexperienced players hit the ball and stop the motion right at the point

Figure 1-14. Reaching for a forehand volley.

of contact. When that happens, the volley lacks pace and will probably serve to set up the opponent for a passing shot.

If your players are having problems at the net, try making a five point checklist. You might even consider placing a one to five value on each of the five points, rating the players, then discussing the ratings with each individual.

Checkpoint:
1. Continental grip; no grip changes; compact backswing.
2. Get the ball before it gets you. Hit everything out in front, and use a forward pivot to get there.
3. Punch the ball from the elbow, and keep the racket head higher than the wrist.
4. Be close to the ball when the volley is hit. No reaching unless absolutely necessary.
5. Follow through, carrying the ball on the strings in the direction you want the ball to go.[4]

THE OVERHEAD SMASH

In considering flaws in the strokes so far, tactics have not been discussed. However, the most common errors made in hitting the overhead smash fall into two categories—tactical and mechanical. The first tactical error is committed because many players do not know whether to hit the overhead while the ball is still in the air or to hit after the ball has bounced. The guidelines covering this decision are simple. If a player can allow the ball to bounce without giving up more than two or three steps toward his own baseline, the ball should be played off the bounce. If, by letting the ball bounce, the player has to retreat more than two or three steps, the ball should be played in the air. If there is a doubt about what to do, the shot should be played after the bounce. The chance for a put-away is less, but the shot will be safer because there is more time to prepare and because the bounce will minimize factors such as wind, velocity, and spin. A simple lob-smash drill in practice should be helpful in teaching inexperienced players how to react to varying types of lobs.

The second tactical error involves when to attempt a put-away and when to go for placement instead of power. Again, the unwritten rule is determined by a player's position on the court more than anything

---

[4]Jim Brown, "Flaw Finish: #5, The Volley" *Scholastic Coach,* in press.

else. If the ball is going to be smashed from a position in the forecourt (from the service line forward), the put-away should be tried, assuming the hitter is capable of putting a ball away. However, if the one preparing to return a lob is close to or behind his own baseline, a put-away smash should never be attempted. The reasons are easy to understand, but some players just cannot resist the temptation to blast every lob, even when the percentages dictate something else. From the baseline, it is very difficult to hit an outright winner. The distance is too far, the angle is poor because of the increased distance, and the opponent has too much time to react. So, instead of hitting an all out smash, the overhead shot should be hit firmly and deeply to an open spot or to an opponent's weakness. If that shot is hit well, the next shot might be a winner.

Probably the most common mechanical error in executing the overhead shot is failure to move the feet during preparation for the shot. Too many players tend to see a lob coming, dig in to a fixed position with both feet, then try to hit. The problem is that since lobs are in the air longer than other shots, all of the variables such as speed, spin, trajectory, and distance may change during the flight of the ball. If a player gets set too soon, he misreads some of the variables and does not adjust his position accordingly. The correction involves having the player take many short, half-and quarter-steps while waiting for the ball. In the same way that a defensive basketball player is constantly shuffling his feet to maintain position, the tennis player should be taking many quick steps to maintain a ready position to hit a smash. As the hit is made, the right-handed player should have planted his right foot to push off and into the ball.

The second mechanical flaw that shows up frequently is an extension of the problem just mentioned. The reason for movement is to assume a position so that when the ball is hit, it is hit in front of the body. The idea is to have the body's weight moving forward as the shot is made. The forward weight shift is easier to accomplish if the target is out in front of everything else. The player in Figure 1-15 is hitting the ball at a point almost directly above his body. As a result his weight is moving back instead of into the ball.

Stand to the side of your players in the lob-smash drill, watching the point of contact. If the player is hitting the ball directly over his head or behind his head, suggest that he point at the ball with the non-racket hand during the backswing. Pointing to the ball might improve concentration, and will make the player more aware of his position in relation to the ball.

Finally, there are many occasions when the overhead smash should be a restricted stroke rather than a full swing. Most teachers instruct

Figure 1-15. Late contact with the ball on an overhead smash.

their pupils to bring the racket directly up in front of the body to a position behind the head as they prepare to hit. A full swing would involve dropping the racket down and bringing it up behind the back in a pendulum-like motion. By eliminating the full swing, the margin of error is reduced. If the position on the court is good, a player should still have enough power to put the shot away or to hit a strong placement. The full swing overhead smash may be more powerful, but it will probably be less efficient and less accurate.

To summarize the problems of the overhead smash, remember that position may be the problem rather than form. Shots should be played properly from a tactical point of view, whether in the air or off the bounce. Next, check the player's position on the court to see that he is trying to put shots away at the right time. If position is not the problem, watch the feet first, the point of contact second, and the type of swing being used last.[5]

[5]Jim Brown, "Flaw Finish: #4, The Overhead Smash," *Scholastic Coach*, 44, no. 8 (April 1975) 15.

THE LOB

Even though flaws are hard to detect when a player is executing a lob, the shot should be discussed here. The lob should be practiced and refined just as other strokes should. The offensive lob should be high enough to clear your opponent's racket if he is at the net and low enough so that he will not have time to run back and play the shot after the bounce. The ball should be placed to an opponent's side. The shot should look like other groundstrokes as far as preparation is concerned. If the shot is not disguised, the opponent will anticipate what is going to happen.

The player hitting a lob must use a lifting motion and a complete follow through. If a flaw in the actual stroke is noticeable, it will probably show up in the follow through. Defensive lobs are difficult to analyze because the player is scrambling and trying to get a racket on the ball in any way possible. You should not be worried about this stroke in terms of spotting a flaw. Just tell your players to get the ball high in the air, put backspin on the shot, and get back to a central defensive position after the shot is made. The idea is to bargain for time and hope for the best.

THE DROP SHOT

As with the lob, the problem with the drop shot is not so much that the technique is wrong, but that the shot is used at the wrong time, not used at all, or that everyone knows that the player is going to attempt the shot. If the coach or teacher can tell when the shot is about to be hit, the opponent certainly should be able to anticipate it. In order not to telegraph the shot, it should look exactly like other shots hit from the forecourt position. This means that there should be no exaggerated backswing, no delay in the stroke, no change in footwork, and no difference in facial expression.

If there are technical problems they will probably fall into one of three categories. First, the trajectory must be so that the ball falls in a more vertical than horizontal plane. For this to happen, the ball must clear the net by a safe margin, not barely skim over the top. Second, the shot must have sufficient backspin to make the ball bite into the court and not travel toward the baseline. The closer it bounces to the net, the less likely it is that the opponent will get to it. Finally, the shot requires touch, and touch requires holding the racket firmly. If the fingers are not securely in touch with the racket handle, the player cannot feel the shot. The idea that the racket should be held loosely on this shot is incorrect. The arm must be relaxed while the grip remains tight.

Checklist for Spotting Flaws

1. Serve
   a. How are the feet aligned in relation to the baseline?
   b. Is a one step or two step approach being used?
   c. Is the toss slightly in front of the body?
   d. Is the toss the right height?
   e. Can the player throw a ball properly?
   f. Is there a rhythm to the swing?
   g. Is concentration a problem?
2. Forehand
   a. When does the player get into a hitting position?
   b. What are the positions of the shoulders and feet?
   c. What is the timing and position on the backswing?
   d. What is the trajectory of the racket as it moves forward?
   e. Is the wrist firm or flexible?
   f. Where is the point of contact in relation to the body?
   g. Where does the racket go on the follow through?
3. Backhand
   a. What is the position of the non-racket hand between shots?
   b. What is the timing and position on the backswing?
   c. Where is the point of contact?
   d. What are the positions of the elbow and shoulder?
   e. Where does the racket go on the follow through?
4. Volley
   a. What kind of grip is being used?
   b. How long or short is the backswing?
   c. Is a forward pivot being executed?
   d. Where is the point of contact?
   e. At what joint on the arm does the primary motion occur?
   f. Is the player reaching for the ball?
   g. Where does the racket go on the follow through?
5. Overhead Smash
   a. Is the ball hit before or after the bounce? Why?
   b. Is the shot put away or placed? Why?
   c. What is the movement of the feet?
   d. What is the position of the body in relation to the ball?
   e. Is a full swing or restricted swing being used?

6. Lob
    a. Is the shot disguised?
    b. Where does the racket go on the follow through?
7. Drop Shot
    a. Is the shot disguised?
    b. Is the trajectory vertical or horizontal?
    c. What kind of spin does the ball have?
    d. Is the racket being held tightly?

2 *Playing Strategies*

DEVELOPING SINGLES STRATEGY

Playing the Odds

Any discussion of developing singles strategy or a game plan for your players has to include comments on percentage tennis. Percentage tennis might also be called smart tennis, efficient tennis, safe tennis, and if properly executed, winning tennis. The concept means that there are certain shots that should be hit in certain situations during the course of a point. If these shots are hit well, the hitter will win that point or be in a position to win the point most of the time. It does not necessarily mean that these percentage shots should be tried 100 percent of the time. If a player falls into a pattern that the opponent can predict, the opponent will have an easier time anticipating the next shot and winning the point himself. Occasionally, hitting the nonpercentage shot will win the point; if not, it will at least keep the opponent honest. However, over a long period of time, hitting the shot that the situation calls for yields positive results. The idea is similar to Vince Lombardi's idea about winning football games. His style was not daring or complex, but conservative and simple. His opponents knew what he would do in most situations, but the execution was so good, there was no way to stop the attack. The tennis player who hits the smart percentage shot is saying, "I'm going to put this shot right where the book says it should go, and there is not much you can do about it."

Playing the odds in tennis requires a disciplined player. First, he has to spend enough time in practice to develop the most efficient shots. For example, the low, down-the-line approach shot does not come automatically. The shot must be practiced repeatedly in order to be used effectively in a match. All the knowledge in the world about smart tennis will not help a player if he cannot hit the required shot when the time comes. If a player is not disciplined enough to spend the hours of practice necessary to perfect percentage shots, he will lose. Second, playing percentage tennis may take some of the fun out of the game for some players. Part of the appeal of tennis is the challenge of making a spectacular shot. Most percentage shots are not spectacular; they are shots designed to set up an opponent for a slow kill. Again, it takes discipline for a player to pass up a chance to hit a great shot in favor of hitting an everyday shot. Some people can never make that adjustment. They are destined to play a few spectacular points or matches, but to lose more than they win over the long run. The challenge for the percentage player is in the winning, not the shot making.

The first rule of percentage tennis is to keep the ball in play. In spite of the pleadings of tennis coaches for decades, most points—75 percent, to be exact—are lost by errors rather than won by good shots. Those statistics imply that teachers and coaches are not doing a very good job of teaching their students to get the ball over the net.

Keeping the ball in play means reducing unnecessary errors. Is there such a thing as a necessary error? There may be, at least in the sense that some errors are forced by an opponent who puts you in a position of trying a difficult shot or hitting an easy set-up. The unnecessary errors that have to be reduced are the kind where the player makes a mistake for no apparent reason. Here are some examples: a player hits a groundstroke into the net or out of bounds while his opponent is in a backcourt position; a player fails to return an easy second serve; a player double faults; a player overhits a smash at the net.

Reducing unforced errors also means taking no needless risks. Players should not try "quarter shots" when "nickel shots" will win the point. If a three-quarter speed serve, deep to the backhand will probably win the point or lead to winning the point, why go for the ace? If a shot that hits three feet inside a line will win a point, why go for the line? If a crisp crosscourt volley wins, why attempt a drop shot? If the difficult shots must be attempted, at least teach your players when to try them. Nonpercentage shots should not be tried unless a player is in a desperate situation during a point or unless he has a comfortable lead in a game or a set. Even then, the low percentage shot can be dangerous. The momentum in a match can change with one shot. Many 40–0 games and 5–0 sets have been lost by the person who had the big lead.

There are specific shots to be hit in playing the tennis odds. Here are some of them:

1. Groundstrokes hit from the baseline should usually be hit crosscourt. The distance from corner to corner is greater than from middle to middle, so the hitter has more space to work with. The net is lower at the middle than at the side, and crosscourt shots will travel over the middle of the net. Crosscourt groundstrokes make the opponent run more and consequently tire more quickly than if given the luxury of returning balls hit down the middle. Crosscourt groundstrokes stay in the air longer, making it possible for the hitter to follow the shots to the net or to have more time to anticipate the returns. Finally, crosscourt shots do not travel close to the alleys, reducing the chance that a mis-hit ball will go out of bounds on the side.

2. Groundstrokes should not only be hit crosscourt, they should also be hit deep into the backcourt of the opponent. Hitting too deeply may be considered a low percentage shot from the standpoint of keeping the ball in play, but the deep shot reduces the opportunity of the opponent to hit an attacking shot on the return. The longer he stays on or behind his baseline, the more time you have to set him up for a forced error or a winning shot.

3. Half court or approach shots should usually be hit down the line. The down-the-line shot should enable the hitter to establish a position at the net so that he can cut off the return. The opponent can either return the shot down the same line or go down the middle. The attacker should be in a position to hit a put-away volley for either shot. It is almost impossible for the opponent to hit a crosscourt shot off of the deep, down-the-line approach shot. His only other alternative is the lob, but the attacker is also in good position to hit the overhead smash. It is important that the down-the-line approach shot be hit deeply, especially on slow courts. If the shot falls short, the opponent can advance into the ball and hit a passing shot. The approach shot should be hit with backspin on the backhand side and with topspin on the forehand side. Mechanically, it is easier to execute the shots in that manner.

4. Volleys should be hit to the open spot on the court or to the opponent's weakness. Just as football players "run to daylight," tennis players should automatically hit where the opponent is not. This usually means hitting crosscourt. There are exceptions, such as when the opponent is anticipating the crosscourt volley and has already started to move in that direction. Then the volley may be hit down the line or down the middle in anticipation of where the open spot will be. Remind your players that the crosscourt volley does not have to hit the line to be a winner. If the first volley is not good enough, the second one should be. If a player stays at the net more than three volleys, the percentages are against him winning the point.

5. First serves should be placed to the outside of the service court in order to pull the receiver off the court. That means that serves will be hit to the receiver's forehand half the time, but if the serve is placed deeply enough or angled sharply enough, the effect of the forehand return will be reduced significantly. The secondary target for first serves is to hit to the opponent's backhand, assuming that the backhand is weaker than the forehand. That is not always true, especially among advanced players. On the left side of the court, both purposes will be served (hitting to the backhand and pulling the receiver off the court) if the ball is placed to the outside of the service court. Just because the first and second choices of targets are dictated by percentages, do not overlook the strategy of mixing up serves in regard to placement, velocity, spin, and capability of the receiver. There are times when variety of attack is just as effective as hitting the textbook shot.

6. Second serves should be hit (a) in, (b) with more spin than the first serve, and (c) as deeply as possible without risking a double fault. Hitting the ball in the service boundaries—keeping the ball in play—is more important than any other consideration. Percentages do not mean anything if the ball is never put into play. Putting topspin on the second serve makes it possible to serve the ball high over the net and at the same time forces the ball to drop in a more vertical trajectory. Both actions result in a safer serve. Putting topspin on the second serve also makes the ball bounce higher, requiring an adjustment by the receiver. Hitting deeply should keep the receiver from hitting an attacking shot on the return.

7. Lobs should be hit to the opponent's backhand side when possible. The high backhand is one of tennis's most difficult shots to handle. If the opponent hits it, the shot cannot have much power. If he runs around the shot, the lobber has time to defend against the overhead smash.

Smart tennis requires that the player avoid going for winners in certain situations:

1. Winners should not be attempted on serves. The odds on hitting aces are slim. The well placed first serve will win the point about 75 percent of the time. The winning shot usually comes on the second or third ball played. The player who goes for the ace throughout the match will wear out sooner, especially on slow courts and in hot weather.

2. Winners should not be attempted on the first groundstroke passing attempt. When the opponent has rushed the net, the first shot at him should be low, firmly hit, and to the opponent's weakest side. The winning shot should be on the next return because the net player cannot do much with a low volley.

3. Winners should not be attempted on approach shots. The idea

is to hit the ball deep and down the line, not to put it away. The put-away follows the good approach shot.

4. Winners should not be attempted on overhead smashes from a position in the backcourt. The opponent has too much time to scramble for a return, the distance is too great, the angle is not good, and the ball stays in the air too long.

5. Winners should not be attempted by hitting drop shots from the backcourt. Again, the ball stays in the air so long that the opponent has time to get to it and perhaps put it away. It is also a low percentage shot because it may be netted.

Learning to Play against Different Styles

An inherent problem in tennis is that players usually practice against the same group of players and learn all of their strengths and weaknesses because of frequent exposure. In a tournament or match the same players have to adjust to a new style within a few minutes. For many players, by the time the adjustment is made, the match is lost. Nothing that anyone can say can completely solve this problem, but there are things that advanced and intermediate players can do to counteract the stereotyped styles among tennis players. Making these adjustments implies that your players are competent enough to make changes and that you or your players are observant enough to recognize a style of play when you see it.

First, consider the big hitter. He probably has the heavy, flat serve, hard groundstrokes, put-away volleys, and the big overhead smash. He likes to serve and rush the net. His asset is power. His weaknesses may be (but not always) lack of patience, mobility, and consistency. It is difficult to consistently move and hit big shots for very long. Your job as a teacher or coach is to prepare your players to take advantage of those weaknesses.

What can your players do about the big serve? They can play a step or two deeper on the return, if necessary. They can block or chip the serve and try to return it low and at the opponents' feet. Big hitters are frequently big people, and it is harder for them to bend their knees to get down on the low volley. In blocking or chipping the big serve, encourage your players to take a short backswing, hold their rackets tightly, and use the pace provided by the serve. The harder the serve is hit, the more the receiver can act as a backboard to reflect the power shots. If your players can get the first serve back in play, the big hitter has lost one of his best weapons. He may also lose his patience later in the match.

What can be done to counteract the heavy groundstrokes? Again, the pace provided by the stronger hitter should be used rather than trying to overpower the power hitter. As much as possible, the returns should force the big hitter to run, hit on the run, bend, stretch, and work hard. All of this should have a cumulative effect of weakening his power shots. He wants to hit a few hard shots and blow the opponent off the court. The opponent wants to keep him on the court and moving as long as possible. The longer he is on the court, the less consistent his big shots should become.

To cope with the strong volleys, make the heavy hitter reach for balls. Make him prove his overhead smash again and again. He will make you look bad on some points, but if that stroke is not solid, it will fall apart later in the match. Make him bend down to hit volleys. Nobody can do much with a low shot at the net. The big hitter will still go for the winner, but his margin of error is small. He could use the drop shot, but big hitters frequently consider that beneath their dignity.

If the big hitter is a superior player, no amount of coaching strategy is going to help your players. If your players have some weapons of their own, however, the big player can be beaten. Slugging matches with him should be avoided by keeping the ball in play, hitting low, and moving the ball around the court as much as possible.

Some tennis players build their games around the big, topspin forehand. It can be a devastating shot, as Laver, Okker, Borg, and Connors have proven. There are ways to minimize the topspinner's attack, but it takes very skillful play.

One tactic—in most cases uncontrollable by the coach or player— is to play this kind of opponent on a fast surface. The extreme topspin requires either a big windup or a quick wrist, and fast courts make balls slide by before the windup is complete or the wrist comes over the top of the ball. Even though coaches and players cannot choose the types of surfaces they prefer, the information about topspins and fast courts can be used to give a psychological boost to someone who is about to play a match.

A second suggestion is to keep the ball deep. This advice is true for almost any kind of player, but it is a must to keep the topspinner from charging, teeing-off with his looping shot, and following it to the net. The deep shot forces the player making the return to retreat and to give up some of the forward motion necessary to execute the topspin forehand. His only other alternative is to attempt a topspin shot off the short hop, which is a low percentage shot.

In addition to keeping the ball deep, the ball should be played to the backhand side of the opponent who uses the topspin forehand. Placing the ball anywhere but on his strong side is good advice. Occasionally, he will try to run around his backhand to hit his best shot. If this happens, he leaves an open spot to shoot for on the return.

To counteract the action of the topspin shot, the player at the baseline must strike the ball while it is on the rise. If not, the groundstroke has to be hit head high, making it a weaker shot from the backcourt, or it has to be hit as the ball descends. Against the good topspin, this means having to retreat well behind the baseline to hit a groundstroke. From this position it is difficult to hit anything but defensive shots.

The retriever or pusher presents a different set of problems. He attempts to get everything back, is a master at keeping the ball in play, and does not try to overpower his opponent. But he has weaknesses also, and here are some ways to take advantage of them.

The retriever has to be moved up and back—from the baseline to the net and back again. The pusher is not usually a strong net player, so he should be brought to the net. To get him there, challenge his ability to hit a strong approach shot. A moderately short groundstroke to either side will force him to come forward. If he does not put the approach away or back your player into the corner, he is probably stuck at the net or in mid-court and may be set up for a passing shot or a lob. If he gets out of that jam, repeat the tactic during the same rally, if possible.

Another possible tactic to use against the pusher is to occasionally overpower him. It is important not to become impatient against this type of player by trying to outpower him more than occasionally. His specialty is getting shots back, and some would be put-aways will come back. Power mixed with short shots, deep groundstrokes, and lobs can be very effective. Anything that will keep him off balance and out of his groove will diminish his chances of winning. The one thing to avoid is playing the pusher's game. He is better at it, conditioned to be on the courts for a long time, and patient enough to let the opponent beat himself.

Playing against lefthanders is a special problem for most players—even lefthanded ones. What can the coach do to prepare his players to fight the southpaw? The first step is to learn the general characteristics of the lefthanded player. The obvious advantage of the lefty lies in his groundstrokes. His characteristics are not different than those of other players, but opponents grooved to hit to the backhand find themselves hitting into a strong forehand. The lefthander knows this and can anticipate what is about to happen. By deliberately leaving a little daylight on the forehand side, he can really suck the opponent into hitting to his strength.

The player who makes a conscious effort can probably adjust to the lefthander at the beginning of points and during low pressure points. But at a crucial moment, he will often forget and revert to his grooved strokes. Only intense concentration throughout the match can help a player avoid this problem.

The lefthander has an even greater advantage on the serve. Most players are not accustomed to the spin produced by a lefthanded serve, which makes the ball bounce to the receiver's left instead of to his right. Some players take the entire match just to figure out the spin and bounce. Practice returning the opponent's warmup serves may partially solve the problem.

The lefthander's serve from the left court also presents a unique problem to the righthander. If the lefthander can serve to the outside of the service court with a spin serve, the combination of trajectory and spin will force the receiver into or beyond the alley for the service return. He also has to make the return with his backhand, which is probably not his strongest shot. The lefty who follows his serve to the net can cheat to his right because of the probable angle of return. The ball should be returned down the line or down the middle; either way, the server has a wide open court in which to hit the follow-up volley. The righthander can reduce the server's advantage by stepping forward rather than to the left on the return, cutting the ball off before it draws him too far off the court.

A third characteristic of the lefthanded player is an apparent preference for hitting the overhead smash to his left side instead of coming across to his right, which should be a more natural motion. No one, not even the lefthander, has explained this wrong side syndrome. He may admit his preference, but he cannot give a reason for it. The righthander can be prepared for the reverse action smash by anticipating it and moving to his right as the ball is hit.[1]

Adjusting to Various Surfaces

The type of surface to be played on should be considered in developing singles strategy. There are too many natural and synthetic surfaces for an analysis of each one. Even with one type of surface there is a wide range. Concrete courts, for example, can be very slow or very slick. Generally, courts are either fast, slow, or in between, and adjustments can be made for at least two of the three.

If a player is going to play a match on a fast surface, he must make these adjustments in planning his strategy:

1. He has to begin his swing earlier than on other surfaces. The ball will bounce low, fast, and tend to slide by unless the racket is brought forward sooner. A shorter backswing than usual may be necessary in order to meet the ball in time and in front of the body.

2. He may have to play deeper than usual, especially on the service

[1]Jim Brown, "Thinking Lefthanded," *Scholastic Coach*, 42, no. 7 (March 1973) 68.

return. The extra step back will give him another fraction of a second to get ready and hit.

3. He can attack on shots that would not be attacking shots on slower surfaces. A better than average serve, volley, or approach shot becomes a great shot if the surface is fast enough. A player can be more aggressive if he can handle the serve and groundstrokes of his opponent.

4. For the reasons just stated, he can expect his opponent to be more aggressive on these courts than on slower courts. He may have to defend against the serve and rush style of play against opponents who would not normally play that way.

For competition on slow surfaces, these changes in style and tactics might work:

1. The player has more time to prepare for shots. He can be more deliberate, wait longer to make a decision about where to hit the ball, and get to balls he would not usually reach.

2. On slow courts, everyone has to be more patient. It takes more time to beat somebody because the ball stays in play longer. The player who wants to get things over with in a hurry will become frustrated on these courts. This is a weakness that should be taken advantage of by the player who takes his time.

3. The server should not wear himself out trying to hit the big serve when playing on these surfaces. The ball is going to bite and slow down when it bounces, so the steam will go out of the hard hit serve. It is better for the server to pace himself for a longer match and to save the big serve for special situations.

4. The server might also consider using a spin serve or an American twist on the slower courts. Because the ball bites into the surface, the effect of the spin will be greater than on faster courts.

5. Slow court players must be very careful about when to rush the net. Even professional tennis players are reluctant to follow a serve on clay courts. Approach shots have to be expertly placed before following the ball into the forecourt. Shallow serves and short approaches turn an offensive tactic into positions of defense.

6. An advanced player might be able to use a topspin groundstroke more frequently on the slow court. There is more time to set up and to bring the racket over the ball. At the same time, he has to prepare to defend against that shot in case the opponent has the same idea.

There is no special advice that can be given for play on "in between" court surfaces. Each player will decide for himself what is fast or slow and must adjust accordingly. For the player with quick reflexes, a strong forearm, and a short backswing, the medium fast surface may play the same as a slow court for other players. Whatever the surface, the best strategy is to try to arrange to practice on it before having to play a match on it.

Putting Everything Together

Developing singles strategy will ultimately come down to what each player can do best on a given day. If he is a pusher at heart, all the strategy you can give him may not help. If a player wants to try big shots and cannot change, there is not much that can be done. Discussions about the most critical points in a game or the most important games in a set are important only in retrospect. The only important points are the one being played next and the last point of a game or a match.

But there are players at the intermediate and advanced levels who can make changes in style or strategy in order to take advantage of a weakness, a strength, or some other factor. Your job is to help him realize when a change should be made and how to make the adjustment.

DEVELOPING DOUBLES STRATEGY

The importance of developing doubles strategy and emphasizing doubles play cannot be overstated. In team competition close matches will always be determined by doubles because they are played after singles matches have been completed. A team can win a majority of singles matches, but lose the team match by scores of 4–3 or 5–4. Doubles play is also important because it helps you to develop a spirit of team unity in what is basically an individual sport. Doubles gives a coach the opportunity to find a spot for almost everyone on the team. If you have more players than positions in the line-up, singles and doubles specialists can be used, especially at the lower spots. Younger players naturally want to play both events, but most coaches would rather have the entire squad partially satisfied than to have one group very happy and the bench warmers ready to quit because they never get to play. Finally, learning to play and enjoy doubles will enable people to use tennis as a lifetime sport. Many players compete in age division singles through the seniors, but most of us drift toward doubles as we get older and slower. The game is still demanding physically, but the older players can use their experience to effectively compete against the younger, stronger players.

Selecting Partners

The most important factor in developing a good doubles team is selecting the people who will play together. It is common knowledge that good singles players are not necessarily good doubles players, so you cannot automatically team up the number one and two players for the number one doubles team, the number three and four players for the number two team, etc. There are several factors to consider in deciding who will play together. First, the partners must be able to get along with each other on and off the court. They must not be the types who will criticize each other verbally or by disgusted looks after lost points. They must be able to accept each other's weaknesses. If they like each other, they can communicate on the court. Some teams communicate verbally by calling for shots, letting the partner know when a lob is about to be put up, shouting a partner off a ball that is going out of bounds, discussing match strategy, and by reassuring each other in difficult situations. Other doubles teams have played together so long or know each other so well, there is very little talking between the two players. Their communication is nonverbal and consists of looks, movements, anticipation, gestures, and shot making. Each method of communication is not only acceptable, but desirable. Doubles is literally and figuratively a team effort; without cooperative effort and understanding, a team has little chance of success even if both players are talented.

A second consideration in choosing partners is style of play. Doubles partners must have games that complement each other. It is usually a good idea to team a power player with a steady hitter. With this combination, one player can take the aggressive role and the other can always see that the team keeps the ball in play long enough to have a chance at winning the point. If two big hitters are teamed together, they are either very good or very bad. When they're hot, they're hot, when they're not, they're terrible. When two retrievers play on the same doubles team, they have trouble putting an opponent away. They invariably find themselves on the baseline playing defensive tennis. If they win, it is because the other team makes errors, not because they win points on the quality of their shots. In doubles, the odds on winning with this style of play are less than in singles competition.

Along with the style of play, each partner must accept and understand his role as part of the doubles team. The steady player must accept the fact that his partner is going to take more chances, hit more winners, and probably make more mistakes. If both players are dashing around like Zorro, nobody is left to mind the store. Taking chances in a doubles match usually leaves a hole open on the court which has to be covered by somebody. The aggressive partner must be disciplined enough to know when to go for big shots and patient enough to give his partner a chance to set him up for the winner. A few players have the ability to be aggressive or to be consistent, depending on the partner's style of play. That player is invaluable as you plan your doubles line up.

Positioning

Most teachers and tennis books promote the idea that there is only one way to play doubles. This is for the partners to play parallel to each other on the court most of the time and to get to the net at the first opportunity. If both players have the skills necessary to play that style of game (deep serves, accurate volleys, and strong overheads), they should stay together and get to the net. But many players cannot play so aggressively or expertly, and the same strategy for them will be disastrous. It makes no sense to serve and rush the net if the server cannot handle himself once he arrives in the forecourt. If one player is good at the net and the other is more comfortable in a backcourt position, it makes sense to play the up and back strategy. If an up and back rotation works for beginners or intermediates, let them play that way. There is always time to evolve into the classic doubles style as each partner develops the necessary skills.

If you can accept the up and back concept for less than advanced players, here are some possible alignments for doubles play. The server will stand half-way between the middle of the baseline and the outside of the alley. The server's partner will stand on the opposite side of the court about a racket's length and a step from the net and approximately one step away from the alley toward the center of the court. After the serve, the server defends his side of the court from the baseline area and his partner protects his side of the court at the net. If the return of serve is lobbed over the net player, his partner will cross over to cover while the net player changes sides of the court in front of him. If the net player poaches to cut off a return, the backcourt player must move in a direction to cover the open court. If the point is not ended with the attempted poach, the net player must position himself on one side of the court rather than staying in the middle. Then his partner will know which side to defend from the backcourt.

The service receiver will stand in front of, on, or slightly behind the baseline (depending on the anticipated velocity of the serve) with one foot within three feet of the inside alley line. If the receiver is the best

net player, he will follow his service return to the net or move toward
the net at the first opportunity. If the receiver's partner is better at the
net, he will station himself on the service line half way between the
middle of the court and the alley on his side. If the return of serve is
either angled sharply or placed deeply, he will advance to the net and
defend his side of the court from a volleying position. If he is not effective
at the net, he should begin the point back on the baseline even with
his partner. As the point is played, he will maintain that position while his
partner waits for an opportunity to move to the net.

Advanced players should have a more structured plan of attack. The
server still lines up on the baseline about half way between the middle
of the court and the alley. When he is serving from his forehand court
(the right court for a righthander) he may serve from a position closer
to the center mark because he can probably cover more open space to his
right with the forehand volley. Following the serve, he advances to a
position on or near the service line for the anticipated crosscourt return.

The server's partner will stand about halfway between the net and
the service line, well inside the alley toward the center of the court. The
exact position depends on the player's preference unless there is some
previously arranged strategy involved. There should be enough room
between him and the alley to tempt the receiver to try a passing shot
down the line, but not enough room for him to make the shot often. By
playing toward the center of the court, the service return will be more
difficult to execute and the server will have less court to cover as the
point progresses. The net player's job is (1) to defend and attack from
his side of the court, and (2) to poach when he can win the point with his
volley. Any time the opponents lob over him, he should cross to the
other side of the court.

The player about to receive the serve will again be in the vicinity
of the baseline. How deep he stands will depend on the surface of the
court and on how hard the server can hit. On the right side of the court,
the receiver will probably play with his right foot very close to or inside
the alley in anticipation of the righthander's serve to the outside of the
service court. On the left side, the receiver can usually play a step
closer to the center because most righthanded servers will have difficulty
serving to the outside. On either side, the receiver can avoid being
pulled off the court to return the wide serve by stepping forward and
into the serve rather than stepping laterally along the baseline. On most
second serves, the receiver should step forward at least one step before
the serve is delivered. The extra step gives him a better position from
which to attack after the serve, it tends to discourage the net player from
poaching, and it can have a psychologically intimidating effect on the
server when he sees the receiver confident enough to move forward to

return his serve. After the serve is returned, the hitter should move in behind his low, crosscourt shot to an attacking position near the service line. If the service return is effective, the opponents should have to volley the ball upward or hit a defensive half volley, setting up the receivers for an offensive volley. What happens after this is unpredictable.

The receiver's partner will begin the point on the service line half way between the middle of the court and the inside alley line. If he is extremely confident of his partner's anticipated return, he may start closer to the net. However, taking a position too close gives the net player a big hole to shoot for if he poaches. Starting the point any further back than the service line is giving up an attacking position. (If the server is especially strong, both receivers may be forced to start from a baseline position.) As the return of serve is made, he advances even closer to the net in a position to cut off the server's second shot. The alley must be protected, so the player may cheat slightly toward the outside of the court on his side. If he does that, his partner can cheat toward the center of the court as he follows his service return in toward the net. It is difficult for an opponent to hit the severe crosscourt shot that would be necessary for a passing attempt.

Righthanders and Lefthanders

If two righthanders play together, the player with the strongest backhand should play the left court. His backhand will be needed for the return of serves to the outside of the odd court. If two lefthanders play together, the opponents could suffer from severe emotional stress. The player with the best backhand should play the deuce court for the reason stated above. The situation is exactly the same, but on the other side of the court. If a righthander and lefthander play together, the righthander should play the right side and the lefthander the left side. They may be weak down the middle where their backhands are, but the benefits of having the forehand crosscourt service returns are greater than the risks of returning shots down the middle.

Playing the Odds

As in the singles game, there are shots that should be hit in certain situations. Here are some of them:

1. First serves should be placed to the outside of the service court, to the receiver's backhand, to an open spot, or occasionally right into his midsection. If those instructions are ambiguous, it is because there are too many variables to say absolutely that "this is where you should serve the ball in doubles." Each target has advantages and disadvantages. Serving to the outside pulls the receiver off the court and reduces his angle of return. Against righthanders playing the right side, the same serve goes into his forehand, which may be his strong shot. Serving to the backhand is usually good percentage tennis, but the returner can hit from a better position and have more alternatives from which to choose. Hitting to the open spot makes sense in any situation except when the opponent has deliberately left a little room, hoping you will hit to his strength. Some players have trouble handling shots hit directly at them, especially if they are expecting the wide serve.

2. Second serves should be hit inside the service court. If that sounds too simple, it is because there is no excuse for double faulting in doubles. The server has to cover only half the court, so he can be more conservative. Serving with topspin will allow him to serve high over the net and will give the server more time to advance toward the net for the next shot.

3. For advanced players, service returns should be hit low and either crosscourt or down the middle. Shots down the middle can be attempted if the net player plays too close to his alley. If the server rushes the net, the idea is to make him bend down and volley up. The speed of the return is not as important as the placement and the low trajectory. If the return clears the net by too much, the serving team can volley down on the ball. The down-the-line return may be used to keep the net player honest, but it is not a percentage shot.

4. Beginners and intermediates should return serves high over the net, crosscourt, and deep (assuming the server does not rush the net). In this situation, the well placed return puts the serving team in a defensive posture.

5. When a player at the net poaches on the return of serve, he should hit to the feet of the receiver's partner. This is the safest, most effective place to hit. It is not unethical tennis. Severe angles and drop shots are more spectacular alternatives for the poacher, but they do not win as many points. The net player should poach when there is a good chance of winning the point or to let the opponents know he is a threat to cut across at any time.

6. After the serve and service return, most shots should be hit down the middle and low. Hitting to the middle can cause confusion about which player will take the shot and draws both players in, leaving more open space for put-aways.

7. On shots hit down the middle, the player with the forehand should make the return. The forehand is usually the stronger shot, and having a predetermined system will eliminate confusion about who is supposed to hit the ball.

8. Percentage doubles for advanced players means getting to the net together and fast. The team that goto theie first should win the point, assuming they are good volleyers. If they are not, they are not advanced players and should be more selective about when to go to the net.

9. The partner with the strongest serve should serve first in every set. By serving first, there is a better chance of getting off to a good start, and the first server will serve more times than his partner in many sets. A possible exception to this rule is when the wind is a factor. The weaker server might have a better chance of holding serve with the wind, while the stronger server can do better against the wind.

10. When the odds do not dictate hitting to a particular spot on the court, hit to the weakest player. If he is significantly weaker than his partner, forget about percentages and play the majority of balls to his side of the court. If his partner tries to cover for him, hit to the place left open.

11. The player serving should call out the score after each point. This suggestion may seem elementary, but high school and college matches have been lost because no one bothered to keep up with the score in a crucial game. Knowing percentages will not help if points are given away by sloppy score keeping.

Mixed Doubles

In tournament or match competition, mixed doubles should be played exactly like any other doubles. There are people who disagree with this concept of the game, but you can read their books to get a dissenting opinion. Serves should be hit with the velocity and to the place on the court most likely to produce a winning point, regardless of race, creed, color, or sex. Shots should be directed to the weakest player on a team. Each player—man and woman—should cover his or her side of the court. The man should not cut in front of his partner unless percentage tennis would call for the tactic in men's doubles. If he poaches too often or hogs groundstrokes, he weakens his team's position by leaving part of the court open for the return. He also demeans his partner. He should pay the consequences for both acts. Given the levels of men's and women's competition today, this philosophy of mixed doubles probably means that the team with the strongest woman will win. More specifically, the team with a woman who can play the net will win if everything else is equal. That is how it should be. If a coach or team enters mixed doubles competition expecting favors from the opponents, they deserve to lose.

CORRECTING COMMON TACTICAL ERRORS

Young, inexperienced players lose matches because of relatively simple errors. Ironically, many tactical errors are made when these players attempt to imitate better, more experienced players. There is nothing wrong with watching players of international tournament level ability and trying to pattern part of your game after theirs. However, the average high school or college player does not have the strength, speed, agility, or background of the world's best players. Therefore, it makes sense for lesser players to adjust their playing strategies to be consistent with their talent and competition. Although it is impossible to define and comment on every possible tactical error made by the beginning or intermediate team player, here are some of the common mistakes the high school or even college coach will see:

Blasting the First Serve

The first serve is probably the most abused offensive weapon in tennis. Too many high school and college players try to knock their opponents off the court with the first serve, then follow it with a very weak second serve. Very few good players hit their first serve as hard as they can. Most use a combination of power and spin, with more power on the first serve and more spin on the second.

Advise your players to sacrifice some power by using two three-quarter speed serves rather than one bomb and one nothing-serve. A well placed, off-speed serve to the opponent's backhand or to an open spot in the service court is just as effective as the attempted ace. The percentages say that the opponent will not return the serve or that it will be returned so weakly that the next shot can be put away for a winner. Once the three-quarter speed serve has been mastered, adding a wrist snap at the peak of the service motion can produce a power serve that will be more than adequate. It should be used sparingly; just often enough to keep the opponent honest.

Spectating

Some players should pay admission to their own matches. They frequently seem to be surprised when a shot comes at them, especially in doubles. The reasons could be lack of concentration, laziness, or just plain admiration of their own last shot. Whatever the reason, the results are disastrous and dangerous.

Teach your pupils to expect every ball to come back at them, regardless of how hard the previous shot was hit or how well placed. They should return to a central position after every shot. By observing an opponent in particular situations, a smart player will learn to anticipate what is likely to happen on the next shot. In doubles, one partner should not look at the other while he is hitting. Instead, the player not executing the shot should have his eyes on the opponents.

Tennis players can learn a lot by watching good baseball outfielders just before a pitch. Although the odds on any one pitch being hit to an area are very low, they crouch, stay up on the toes, and spring forward on each pitch. They expect every ball thrown to be hit directly to them. In tennis, the odds are at least even that every shot you hit is going to come back at you. Better to hit it than to eat it.

Rushing the Net at the Wrong Time

Many inexperienced players use a suicide strategy in charging the net. For apparently self-sacrificial reasons, they rush forward during a point courageously, but futilely. Others try to sneak up to the net as if to surprise their opponents (following a weak second serve, for example). The opponent will certainly be surprised, and very pleasantly so, because it is easy to pass this misguided human missile.

The young player should not rush the net at all unless he can handle the situation once in the forecourt. If a player can play the net, he should rush only when the opponent is at a disadvantage; that is, after hitting a shot deep to the backhand, pulling him off to one side of the court, or after lobbing over his head. The only time an opponent should be surprised is when he turns around after chasing down a well placed, angled, deep shot, and sees you at the net ready for a put-away volley.

Playing Too Far from the Net

Many high school players seem to think that by not crowding the net, they are improving their chances for a return. Some are afraid to get too close to the net for fear of being hit, and others are afraid of being passed.

The farther back from the net a player stands, the greater the margin of error on volleys. Standing too far back can result in shots that dribble off the racket and into the net, and it gives the opponent more time to react to the volley when the shot does clear the net. World class players stand in the area of the service line, but remember that their skills are vastly different than the average school player.

Suggest that your players begin by standing a racket's length and one step from the net. Once he feels comfortable at that distance, he can move back to a position in which he can cover more territory. Until that level is reached, it is better to keep the young player close to the net. Some points will be lost because of passing shots and lobs, but others will be won because of a better attacking position and a better position from which to deflect shots that would not have made it over the net from a position nearer the service line.

Playing the Big Game

Aspiring players watch their tennis heroes for pointers. However, many established players are using a serve, rush, and volley type of game which most high school and some college players cannot play effectively. When they attempt the same kind of strategy, a tragedy of errors usually follows. At most levels, points, games, and matches are lost rather than won. Most high school players who rely on big shots to win, will not.

Tell your players to keep the ball in play. This does not mean just pushing the ball back, but using sound, crisp groundstrokes mixed occasionally with the big shots. Tennis games should be built from the baseline forward. Young players should develop reliable serves, forehands, and backhands before concentrating on volleys, overhead smashes, and other put-away shots. A solid game from the baseline will force an opponent into game losing errors and set you up for game winning big shots as a match progresses.

Trying to Look Good Rather Than Playing to Win

This problem is closely related to playing the big game. Too many players feel that if you do not play the big game, you are pushing, and pushing is a dirty word in tennis circles. Pushing, to some, is playing sissy tennis. Others do not seem to care whether they win or lose, but how they look to the crowd. These players are well known for looking sensational during the warmup, but falling apart once the match begins. To add to the problem, they keep convincing themselves that their game is just "off" when they lose. To be more accurate, their true game is "off" when they win, which is seldom.

Athletes should play to win. Forget what the books say about clothes, some tennis etiquette, and how the pros play the game. Within the bounds of efficient form, good players develop their own styles of hitting. Most of the top players in the world have peculiarities about their games not found in tennis textbooks. Yet, these men and women have reached the top because they use the form that suits their size, strength, quickness, and philosophy of tennis. If pushing wins, push. If scrambling wins, scramble. If hitting a two handed backhand wins, do it. If just looking good on the court is not enough to win, forget about looking good.[2]

ADJUSTING TO WIND, SUN, AND HEAT

Fair weather tennis players complain about the wind, the sun, and the heat; they stall, they look disgusted, they do not enjoy themselves, and they frequently lose. Tennis is not as enjoyable when the weather is not perfect, but all players have to play in less than perfect conditions sooner or later, so it makes sense to learn to adjust to the elements rather than lose to them. Here are some suggestions you can give your students or team members to make that adjustment:

Playing When the Wind Is a Factor

1. Toss the ball lower than usual on the serve. Lowering the toss reduces the margin of error because the ball tends to move with the wind on a higher toss, causing a last second adjustment in the service motion.

2. Do not attempt drop shots when the wind is at your back. The wind can turn what would have normally been a winning drop shot into a floater which your opponent has time to get to and put away.

3. Keep lobbing to a minimum. It is simply too risky on a windy day, especially if the wind is gusting. If you must lob, use a highly arched defensive lob when with the wind, and a hard, topspin, low offensive lob against the wind.

4. When with the wind, play a step or two closer to the net in most situations (especially on the service return). When you are against the wind, play slightly deeper than usual. One exception is when you are serving with a strong wind at your back. If the serve tends to go deep, try standing a step behind the baseline.

5. Take more chances when playing against the wind. Shots that would normally be too high, too hard, or too deep often drop in against the wind. You cannot play a normal groundstroke game against the wind. You must force the action or be blown off the court by your opponent or the wind.

6. Conversely, play more conservatively with the wind. Shots that would usually be safe placements become winners when extra pace is provided by the wind.

[2]Jim Brown, "Seven Cardinal Sins of High School Tennis Players," *Scholastic Coach*, 41, no. 7 (March 1972) 68.

7. When playing doubles on a windy day, let the partner with the more powerful serve go against the wind while the weaker server uses the wind to make his serve stronger. If there is no difference between the two, let the weaker net player be at the net when his partner serves with the wind. This forces the opponents to return serves against the wind, slowing the ball, and giving the weaker net player more time to react.

8. Before the match begins, consider using your alternative on the racket spin to play against the wind during the first game. Even if your opponent wins his serve, you change sides after the first game and have the wind at your back for two consecutive games.

Playing When Looking into the Sun Is a Hazard

1. When serving, toss the ball farther to either side of the head than usual, or toss the ball behind the head to avoid looking into the sun. When either of these variations is used, the ball must be served with an unusual amount of spin. Although both serves may be effective, serves with spin have less velocity than flat serves. This means the opponent has more time to react to your serve, but it also gives you more time to establish a position when rushing the net.

2. If you are playing against the sun and depend on a serve and volley game, consider that any lob your opponent hits is going to force you to look into the sun. On the other hand, if your opponent comes to the net, give him more than his quota of lobs when he is on the sunny side. He is trying to gain an advantage by cutting down the size of the court, so there is nothing unethical about making him pay for his aggressive behavior.

3. In doubles, two righthanders may have varying service styles, so that one is less affected by playing the sun court than the other. This factor should be considered at the beginning of the match when the order of serving is established. If a lefthander and righthander play together, a rotation can be arranged so that neither has to be bothered by looking into the sun while serving.

Playing When the Temperature and Humidity Are High

Although high temperature and humidity create obvious problems, many tournament players disregard both factors until it is too late. The price they pay is a lost match or a less effective performance in subsequent matches. Generally, the bigger a player's game, the more likely he or she is to wilt under the sun. It is very difficult to teach someone to pace himself, but these ideas might help:

1. Be careful about using a maximum velocity serve during the first set. While the big serve might win some early battles, it takes so much out of a player that the war might be lost later. If the big server does not win the match in two sets, he will be in trouble in the third.

2. Select some times during a game to serve and stay in the backcourt. Points can be won without serving and rushing. It is very demanding for a player to serve and rush fifty times in one set even under normal conditions. The longer the match lasts, the more fatigued the net rusher becomes, the less he advances toward the net, and the weaker his volleys become. Put them all together and you lose in three sets.

3. Although easier said than done, make your opponent move around the court. Now is not the time to blast him off the court, but to run him so much that he leaves voluntarily.

4. Keep the racket handle dry. How? With commercial products, hand towels, several wrist bands, by alternating rackets every two or three games, and by carrying the racket in the nonracket hand between points. This not only helps to keep the handle dry, but it also reduces fatigue in the muscles of the racket hand and forearm.

No suggestion is going to enable a weak player to beat a strong player. But if everything else is equal, knowing how to play in all kinds of weather can give your player an advantage.

LEARNING TO ANTICIPATE

The intermediate tennis player is often faced with a frustrating problem. He has developed his strokes so that he appears to be as good as advanced players; he has started to develop his own game plans rather than being forced into a style of play by his opponent; however, he loses to some players of seemingly equal talent because he does not yet know how to anticipate what is about to happen during a point. His opponents know what he is going to do before he does it, and when he thinks he has the advantage in a particular situation, he loses points because he has been "out-anticipated."

Much of what players and coaches refer to as anticipation is learned through years of experience. If a player learns the game before he is fifteen years old and continues to play regularly, by the time he reaches the junior veteran classification, he has had twenty years of seeing shots and being in every conceivable court situation. It is for this reason that older doubles teams can defeat younger players even though the youngsters have the physical edge.

However, the intermediate player, whether in high school, college, or out of school, can do three things to make up for the anticipation gap. He can learn basic tennis strategy; he can familiarize himself with his opponent's playing habits; and he can watch for tip-off signs.

If a player knows basic tennis strategy, he should know what most intermediate or advanced players do in a given situation. In other words, what do the principles of sound tennis dictate in this situation? Here are a few examples of percentage shots: (1) Volleys hit following the serve will be placed deep and cross-court. (2) Approach shots will usually be hit down the line. (3) First serves will usually be placed to the outside of the service box in order to pull the receiver off the court. (4) Second serves will be hit with less velocity, but more spin. (5) Offensive lobs will usually be placed to the opponent's backhand side.

If a player is familiar with his opponent's playing habits, he can make a relatively accurate guess about what he usually does in this particular situation. Almost all players have a favorite side or a favorite shot. Intelligent players will scout their opposition and make mental notes about individual idiosyncrasies, strengths, and weaknesses. If the match is against an unfamiliar opponent, your player can usually talk to someone who has played against him. Some coaches require their players to make written scouting reports after each match.

Assuming that the player in question knows some basic tennis strategy, and after he has gathered all the information possible about an opponent, he is still faced with the most important, immediate question: What is my opponent going to do on this shot? It is in this area that a coach can make suggestions that may be helpful. These suggestions will not replace twenty years of experience, but they cut the gap down enough to make a significant difference in winning or losing some matches.

Watch the opponent's eyes prior to the serve.

Many players, even those in the advanced group, inadvertently look at the spot where they plan to serve immediately before the toss. If a receiver is watching his opponent's eyes closely enough, he can detect this tip-off sign and adjust accordingly. It may mean moving a step or two to the right or left, changing from one grip to another, or doing nothing, but having more confidence and purpose in the service return. Whatever it does for a player, it gives him an advantage in games many players expect to lose; that is, games where the opponent is serving.

Watch the opponent's feet as he prepares to hit groundstrokes.

A closed stance (one in which the feet are more or less parallel to the alley) usually indicates that the next shot is more likely to go down the line or straight ahead than anywhere else. An open stance (one in which the foot closest to the net does not come around to the parallel position) might be a tip-off that a cross-court shot is coming. On the serve, if the opponent's feet are pointing straight to the baseline, expect a flat, hard serve. If the feet are pointing to the side of the court, watch for the twist.

Watch the opponent's racket head as the backswing is taken.

If the racket head starts low and moves in a vertical motion rather than a motion horizontal to the court, watch for the topspin shot. When a shot is hit with topspin, the sound will be the same and the motion just as rapid, but the shot will have less velocity than a flat shot, it will rise fast, drop fast, and then take an unusually high bounce. If the racket head is drawn straight back, the return is likely to be flat, with good pace, and low to the net. If the racket head goes back high, watch for the chop (underspin). The chop will float a little, bounce lower than other shots, and slow down or bite into the court when it bounces.

Watch the ball—even when it is on the other side of the net.

All tennis players have been taught to keep their eyes on the ball as they hit. Few have been taught to watch the ball as the other player prepares to hit. For example, when a righthanded player serving from the right side tosses the ball up on the right side of his body, he is likely to serve closer to the middle of the court. If he tosses the ball across his body to the left, watch for the serve to go to the outside of the service court.

Watch how the ball bounces prior to the opponent's groundstrokes. The ball may slide as it bounces, causing him to hit up. It may hit a line, crack, or object on the court, throwing his timing off. The ball may bounce closer to him than he expected, usually causing him to hit up, without an angle, and with a lack of pace.

Be aware of the court position of the opponent.

A player can do only certain things in certain situations. As an example, a player is at the net, and hits a short volley. His opponent is well back in the court and has to charge forward and stretch to reach the ball. In this situation it is practically impossible to pick the ball up enough to clear a player who is standing at the net. The player who made the volley can move in even closer to the net and expect the shot to come at him head high.

Another example is when the player is at the net and the opponent lobs over his head. As he goes back to play the lob off the bounce, he should sneak a glance at the opponent. Is he standing still? Is he rushing the net, or just loafing in? Running back and looking over the shoulder instead of at the ball may be the epitome of optimism, but it is worth the effort if it wins one point per match.

A third example is when the opponent is at the net, and the player attempts a lob to his backhand side. If the lob is high enough to make him stretch, but not high enough to clear him, the chances are good that he will go cross-court with his volley. Although there are exceptions to this probability, the player can take a chance and make an early move in the proper direction, hopefully making a winner out of the next shot.

Careful observation of these tip-off signs, combined with knowledge of tennis strategy and of an opponent's habits, will enable the intermediate player to make a good guess about what is going to happen in many situations. Anticipation requires as much or more concentration as hitting the ball. Decisions based on partial evidence must be made in fractions of seconds. But partial evidence is better than no evidence at all, and by anticipating a shot, a player can move into position and get the racket ready a few seconds sooner. These few seconds are precious, and become increasingly more precious as a player improves and meets better competition.[3]

Figures 2-1 and 2-2 illustrate how watching an opponent's racket head and feet might indicate where the next shot will be hit. In Figure 2-1, the player's racket head is high on the backswing—a sign that the shot will be hit with backspin. His feet are in a closed stance, indicating that the ball will probably be hit straight ahead or down the line. In Figure 2-2, the racket head appears to be starting forward from a lower position, which usually tips off the opponent that a topspin shot is coming. The open stance, in this case shown by the lefthander's right foot, could mean that the shot will be hit crosscourt.

Figure 2-1. High backswing indicates the shot will be hit with backspin; closed stance usually indicates that the ball will be hit straight away or down the line.

[3]Jim Brown and Brian Chamberlain, "Anticipation and the Intermediate Tennis Player," *Athletic Journal*, 51, no. 9 (May 1972) 38.

Figure 2-2. Low backswing precedes a shot with topspin; open stance could mean the shot will be hit crosscourt.

3 Teaching The Game

TEACHING CHILDREN

It is exciting and gratifying to see so many smooth-stroking, court-wise tennis players under the age of twelve. But it is also misleading. Whenever we see a ten-year-old serving, stroking, and volleying like an adult, we probably assume he or she is also thinking like one.

With due respect to the intellect and judgment of the twelve and under age group, it is important to remember that their approach to the game and their technical problems are different from those of older groups. These differences must be recognized in order to ensure the proper psychological approach during the formative years.

All of us have psychological needs. Perhaps the four most basic needs are (1) the need to belong, (2) the need for security, (3) the need for recognition, and (4) the need for love. Each of these needs must be satisfied, and they can be partially satisfied by participating in a well conducted program of tennis instruction.

Young players usually need to belong—to be part of a group. Initially, the group may consist of only two people: the instructor and the student. If you are the instructor, you may have to sell yourself to the student before you can begin selling the game. You must have the kind of personality attractive to children, and by now you know whether you do or do not.

Learning to play tennis can be difficult and frustrating, especially to children who have not matured physically or emotionally. The typical under-twelve-year-old beginner has little chance of immediate success in mastering the skills of the game. He or she must be attracted to the peripheral aspects of the sport such as the instructor, the other players, the lead-up games, and the total tennis program (lessons, competition, work, recreation, fellowship, and related social activities).

Once an interest in the game has been instilled in the young player, you must wean him away from you and encourage participation with a peer group of players. The mother who brings her boy or girl to the courts and waits while he or she takes a lesson cannot expect that child to become much of a tennis player. Children in the seven to eleven age group have a strong need for group associations. Since tennis is primarily an individual activity, the group need must be satisfied in some other manner. It is an excellent idea for a group of friends to go to the courts together, play together, and go home together. The most valuable contribution that the instructor can make with respect to the need to belong is to push the reluctant beginner forward and to develop his skills so that the other young players will want him to be part of their group.

Although all of us are insecure in one way or another, no one is more insecure than the eight year old who is hanging on to a racket almost as big as he is, while attempting to defend himself against balls which are attacking him and trying to master a game that 99 percent of the people in the world has failed to master. With the young player facing such overwhelming odds, the instructor has an obligation to provide a little security and stability for his student. The child's relationship to adults is very important in satisfying this need, and the tennis instructor is one of those adults who can play a definite role.

The instructor should know every pupil by his or her first name, he should know something about the child's interests other than tennis, and he should know about the child's family. The instructor should maintain a regular schedule of lessons so that a child knows that he or his group will get special attention at least during that time period. The instructor should be there for scheduled lessons, not delegate the teaching to someone else. The teacher's actual approach to learning is important. Educational research shows that youngsters prefer teachers who are fair, firm, consistent, and friendly. All of these qualities will make the beginning tennis player more secure as he learns the game.

You can criticize Little League Baseball for many things, but you must admit that much of its success stems from the recognition given to the players. They have uniforms, coaches, sponsors, leagues, publicity, awards, ballparks, and other fringe benefits that attract kids to the game. Since tennis is an individual sport, not as well organized at the junior level, and more difficult to publicize than baseball, the instructor is again called upon to help satisfy a basic need—recognition. There are both subtle and direct means of providing recognition for those who need it.

Children have a powerful desire to be first, to be noticed, and to be singled out for attention. A simple statement such as, "Amanda hit that forehand better than I could have hit it," made in front of a group may be the equivalent to the Wimbledon trophy for many beginners. Other forms of recognition such as applauding a good shot, paying attention to a student's match, and giving students bulletin board publicity also serve as valuable psychological tools. Giving expensive trophies as a method of recognition is overdone, but awards such as certificates, ribbons, medals, and prizes can be used effectively to reward and recognize students' achievements in practice as well as in tournaments and matches.

Finally, everyone—adults, adolescents, and especially those in the seven to eleven group—needs love. In the instructor-student relationship, it is a very simple kind of love which means, "I trust you," "I know you can do it," or "Let's figure out how we can solve this problem together." It is the kind of love that develops out of mutual interest and the mutual challenge to achieve a goal.

A good tennis instructor should be just as interested in teaching tennis as the pupil is in learning to play. If not, his lack of interest in and understanding of his pupil will be evident. The beginner will either lose interest in the game or he will find another instructor. It is difficult for some people to recognize that when a tennis instructor goes to the courts, he is going to work, not to play. But even though the teacher's work is somebody else's play, the instructor has to enjoy or perhaps even love that work. If he does, some of that love will rub off on those he teaches. Here are other psychological approaches to teaching tennis to the elementary age group:

1. Develop standards of achievement based on an individual rather than a group rate of improvement. Consider the readiness factors (physical, mental, and emotional) in each student.

2. Provide an opportunity for success regardless of the child's ability. Hitting five forehands over the net in a row could represent enough success to keep a seven year old coming back for more instruction and play. Eve Kraft's *Tennis Workbook* offers excellent ways of setting reasonable goals and measuring a player's success.

3. See that young players enjoy the activity that tennis provides. Playing tennis beats standing in right field for two hours, butting heads at left tackle, and running a mile. Kids enjoy hitting a ball over a net, and the instructor should see that they get to do that frequently and with a minimum of standing around waiting. Two other suggestions: (a) make sure that your students achieve a degree of skill at a technique before going on to something new, and (b) stop the practice of an activity while the interest is still high. This will guarantee some enthusiasm the next time the activity is presented.

4. Tell students why you are asking them to do whatever they are doing. Many teachers never explain, probably because they do not know the reasons for tennis mechanics themselves. For the elementary group, a detailed explanation is not necessary. A simple, direct statement or answer is enough. Too much explaining will provide more information than most children care to have.

5. If practical, it may be wise to separate boys and girls in some competitive lead-up activities. In the nine to twelve age group, the girls will out-achieve the boys frequently, and "Women's Lib" notwithstanding, nothing will turn a male chauvinist boy off of an activity quicker than being beaten by a girl. You can argue that society should not support that kind of thinking, but you must then decide whether you want to be a crusader or to hold on to all of your students.

The better tennis instructors have learned these psychological principles through training and experience. Unfortunately, there are many young instructors with good tennis skills but little or no background in psychology or physical education. In order to be effective with any age group, the teacher must have a combination of technical ability and an understanding of people. If mistakes are made with children trying to learn the game, they may quit and never return.[1]

TEACHING ADOLESCENTS

No other age group has been written about more than the adolescents. Articles and books are seldom seen about people in their twenties, forties, or sixties, but everybody seems to have opinions about the attitudes and behavior of adolescents, especially the specific group in that range known as teenagers. Parents have trouble communicating with them. Colleges offer courses in adolescent psychology to study them. Children idolize them. Are adolescents different from any other segment of the population? Most psychologists agree that they are different.

For example, there are three stages of adolescence: preadolescence, which begins to appear in nine and ten year olds; adolescence, which begins at about twelve years and continues to emerge until the late teens, when the late adolescence period starts. The lines dividing these phases are vague. They may not be consistent from person to person, or the same person may develop different characteristics at various times during the entire age span.

Adolescents are different because our society expects and even forces

[1]Jim Brown, "Psychological Factors in Teaching Tennis to Pre-Teens," *Scholastic Coach*, 41, no. 8 (April, 1972) 104.

them to be different. As a result, they have social, emotional, and physical problems not characteristic of other groups. The tennis teacher or coach has to take these differences into account in order to be effective in working with this age group. This part of the book will point out some of the special problems teaching adolescents presents and suggest ways to solve these problems.

Grouping

Whether you are teaching a physical education class, coaching a team, or working in some other instructional capacity, you are going to have to make some decisions about grouping players for instruction, practices, or recreational tennis. There are several factors to consider when you start grouping adolescents. One factor is grouping by sex. The early adolescent, roughly those in the ten to thirteen age group, will probably feel more comfortable working in a group of his or her own sex. Since girls tend to mature physically and emotionally a little sooner than boys, the girls might be more at ease in a mixed group. They will probably be more skilled in tennis, also. But the boys generally want to be with other boys, to compete against other boys, and not to be compared to girls in any way. As both groups move into the middle adolescent years, it will be easier for you to mix them in various tennis activities. During late adolescence, you may even have to segregate them by sex again to get anything done as far as serious tennis is concerned.

Grouping by ability is important for several reasons. The emphasis on individualized instruction in the schools necessitates designing instruction for each student. You cannot accomplish much if there are beginners, intermediates, and advanced players in the same group. You will be underteaching some and teaching over the heads of others. The advanced players will be bored, the beginners will be intimidated and possibly discouraged from coming back, and the intermediates will be looking over their shoulders to see what is going on with the other two groups. As much as possible, keep the three levels in separate units with activities designed for their skill levels. If students of varying abilities must be mixed because of time or space limitations, use practice drills in which one group can be used to set up shots for another. Advanced players may also be used to help you teach basic skills to beginners.

Grouping by age and particularly by grade in school is a factor to consider, especially in urban areas. Our system of education emphasizes highly graded schools. One of the results is that many students prefer to study, work, socialize, and play tennis with other students their age or in their grade. Since adolescents will develop their tennis skills at varying rates, some mixing of age groups is inevitable. But if there are problems of motivation, communication, or students getting along with each other, at least consider the possibility that age grouping might be the cause.

The last problem with grouping is to separate those who want to play the game seriously from those who want to play "giggle tennis." There is a place for those who just want to play for the fun of participating without being overly competitive or very serious about the game. They should be provided with a program that will meet their needs, and the first essential of that kind of program is to find others who are looking for the same thing. Those who want to play tennis for the sake of competition, rapid improvement, and recognition must have a more rigorous regimen of practicing, playing, and conditioning. The two groups are vastly different and should be separated on the courts.

Making Tennis Fun

Adolescents are frequently looking for experiences that will help them to learn more about themselves. They are rehearsing for roles they may have to play later in life. In our society, boys have traditionally tried to compete in sports requiring skill, strength, and sometimes courage. In the past, girls have been more interested in developing social skills, but that concept is changing. The continuing emergence of women as participants in all areas of endeavor has been a tremendous boost to the increased interest in tennis. It is no longer unfeminine to run, jump, work hard, and perspire. The change in values means that women are a vast natural resource for participation in all athletics, and especially in tennis.

With these concepts in mind, it is the responsibility of the tennis instructor to attract people to the game. It is time for tennis to stop losing the best athletes to football, basketball, baseball, drill squads, and social clubs. The best way to attract players is to make the sport attractive and fun. Here is a quick review of some tennis selling points: (1) It is good for health and fitness, as evidenced by the fact that you can build strength and burn as many as six hundred calories an hour simultaneously. (2) Tennis can be used for social purposes by introducing the player to a new group of friends. (3) Compared to other sports, tennis is a time-saving way to get a workout. Playing an hour of tennis is equal to several hours of playing golf, bowling, or playing most positions in baseball. (4) Tennis is economical when compared to other activities. A person can get started with an investment of ten to twelve dollars. Compare that with the cost of golf clubs, hunting and fishing equipment, or football gear. (5) Tennis is a lifetime sport. When the last high school or college football game is over, some athletic careers end. Those who have been playing tennis are just getting started. (6) Tennis can be a tough, challenging, competitive sport for those who want it to be. In a list of all the physical and mental qualities necessary to play the various sports popular in this country, tennis will be near the top. For the high school athlete trying to withstand the pressure of friends, parents, and coaches who want him to play another sport, try showing him the list of skills and appeal to his athletic spirit. The list could include speed, strength, endurance, power, flexibility, reflexes, ability to stop and start quickly, ability to make split second decisions, ability to track and hit a moving object, ability to perform alone in singles and with a partner in doubles, etc. Again, tennis will compare favorably with any other sport. (7) Tennis is fun. It beats most of the other sports for pure enjoyment, and it really beats them in that it can be just as much fun to practice as it is to play. This is where the good instructors are separated from the bad ones.

It is your job to make sure the adolescent enjoys playing tennis. If he does not, there are many alternative activities competing for his attention. Classes, lessons, or practice sessions for the teenager should involve activities in which he can enjoy himself and at the same time improve his skills. This does not mean that practicing and playing is not hard work. It just means that anybody can enjoy working hard. The work-enjoyment combination requires a teacher who is capable of planning and directing activities to fill both needs.

Keeping Them Busy

If there is one almost universally recognized characteristic of the adolescent, it is his restlessness. It is almost torture to make a teenager stand in line, sit and listen to a lecture, or to be part of anything passive. The message for the tennis instructor is to keep them busy. Have something for them to do every minute they are under your supervision. If they are not hitting, they can be throwing to someone else. If they are not throwing, they can pick up balls. If there are no balls to pick up, they can be running or doing weight work. If nothing else, they can keep charts on players. Work them to death. If you allow them to sit around doing nothing (except during required recovery periods after intense work), you are not only wasting their time, you are probably giving them a chance to get into or give you trouble.

Recognizing Physical Changes

Remember that the adolescent is undergoing a period of rapid and sometimes difficult physical changes. His tennis thinking may be ahead of his physical capabilities. He will want to try shots that his body will not let him make consistently. It is your job to be patient with the awkward teenager, to be understanding with the adolescent who does not experience the rapid growth changes, and to challenge the physically gifted students. To do the job effectively, you will again face problems of individualizing instruction to meet everyone's needs.

Providing a Role Model

The typical adolescent is uncertain of his status. He is making the trip from childhood to adulthood, and he is not sure how he is supposed to behave in between. He will complain that his parents do not understand him and that they treat him like a child, but he is not yet ready to assume all the responsibilities of living as an adult. He certainly needs adults to look up to in addition to his parents, and the teacher or coach fulfills that need. Be professional in your behavior around students without being aloof. Be friendly without being their buddy. Most important of all, give them opportunities to work, play, compete, socialize, and enjoy themselves in a way that will help them grow into maturity.

Acknowledging Intellectual Ability

In spite of all his seemingly strange behavior, do not overlook the fact that the adolescent is quite capable of handling himself intellectually. In fact, intellectual capacity peaks during adolescence. Applied to tennis, this means the average teenager can understand tennis tactics and strategy and their relationship to his game. Unfortunately, the intellectual ability to recognize the importance and logic of strategic tennis is offset by the lack of playing experience. Dumb players who play the game long enough eventually develop some sort of game plan. Bright young tennis players will develop a thoughtful approach sooner. The teacher should be able to talk with the adolescent student about game strategy and mechanics of strokes. Eventually, the body will catch up with the mind.

Remembering Uniqueness

Now that you have read about all of these adolescent characteristics, forget them for a minute. Keep in mind that each person, regardless of age, is unique. There are teenagers who exhibit every trait just discussed; there are others who do not fit into any category. Some will be physical adults and emotional children. Others will be just the opposite. Know your students well and you can design your teaching to fit their personalities and capabilities.

TEACHING ADULTS

As tennis continues to gain popularity, increasing numbers of people are showing up at public parks, college courts, and tennis clubs looking for someone to teach them how to play the game. Many of these people have discovered tennis in their twenties, thirties, and forties, and are "over-the-hill" as far as serious competitive tennis is concerned.

The lack of background and experience in the sport does not make these new players any less enthusiastic about the game. On the contrary, like those converted to a new religion, they are the true tennis zealots. They play in the worst weather; they bother better players trying to get a match; and they probably do more to promote tennis than most club pros.

However, the late blooming tennis player presents certain problems to the teacher. There are psychological approaches that work with younger players that should be avoided with the older group. There are also teaching techniques applicable to this group which would not be appropriate at any other age level.

First, the instructor must be able to do a lot more explaining with beginning adults than with younger players. A ten year old will move his or her feet because you tell him to; a thirty-five year old housewife wants to know why moving her feet is necessary to hit the ball with a racket. Sometimes, this kind of questioning separates the real tennis teachers from the pseudo-instructors who go through the motions, but haven't the faintest idea of why some things work and some do not.

Second, the over-the-hill gang needs constant positive reinforcement about its collective game. Inexperience combined with a late start breeds insecurity, and insecure is what any tennis player should not be. The instructor should be honest and not lead an inept player into thinking he is a champion, but he should also compliment his students frequently and so that others can hear. Telling a middle aged accountant that his last forehand shot was the best you have seen all day may mean that all the others have gone into orbit, but the compliment is still worth giving.

Many players in the adult group have had some playing experience before they take lessons from a tennis pro. The experience was probably just enough to really ruin their opportunity to develop good strokes, but there is a chance that they are doing some things successfully, if not technically sound. It is best to leave that part of their game alone. If a stroke is successful, it matters little how it looks. The professional ranks are full of players with styles not described in instructional articles and books. Besides, the older beginners need a security blanket to fall back on, and that weird looking backhand may be that blanket.

The older "gang" can be divided into two groups. One group is made up of young Turks who are learning fast, improving every time they play, and playing almost every day. The other group is likely to be older, not really sure whether or not they are going to make it, and not able to play frequently. Here are some suggestions for instructors who have players in the second group:

1. Do not expect these players to take lessons as regularly or to practice as frequently as other learners. Many of them have too many business and social commitments to play as much as they should.

2. Teach the slower adult learners at a slower rate than the more aggressive group. Settle for one new stroke or situation per lesson, and give the student ample time to practice what he or she has learned.

3. Encourage your less skilled pupils to play doubles with other players of equal ability. This will let them see that others are having similar problems, and it also makes the game a more socially pleasant experience, which is what many players want as much as winning trophies.

4. Make sure that the learner gets to hit with someone who can keep the ball in play. Nothing is worse than two people hitting against each other when three consecutive balls over the net is about the most they can hope for. That kind of practice becomes an exercise in chasing balls, and it should be avoided as much as possible.

5. Face the fact that there are some things that older, slower players will never be able to do. It will be frustrating for the teacher and the player, but both may have to accept the fact that certain players are never going to have a sensational backhand or a strong second serve.

6. Teachers of adult beginners should be particularly sensitive in their on-the-court relationship with the player. It takes a lot of courage for someone to try to learn a sport when children half your size and one-fifth your age are on the next court smashing shots and making it look easy. This kind of courage should be rewarded with understanding, patience, and a maximum effort by the teacher. If he does his job properly, he will be a better teacher from having learned from his pupil, and tennis will have gained a solid follower.[2]

[2]Jim Brown, "Newcomers to Tennis Instruction are Often Oldtimers," *Tennis Trade*, 2, no. 4 (April, 1973) 32.

TEACHING PRIVATE AND GROUP LESSONS

In this chapter the phrase "Teaching Private and Group Lessons" means teaching individuals or small groups and being paid for the lessons. The fact that the teacher will be paid directly by the students or their parents imposes a kind of quality control on instruction. You must either have a monopoly on the tennis teaching market in your area or you must give your clients their money's worth. If not, you will be out of business just like any other businessperson. Here are some ideas on how to operate your tennis teaching business effectively and profitably.

Attracting customers is the first priority. If you have established a reputation as a player or teacher, people will come to you. If not, newspaper advertisements, radio-television spots, and bulletin board posters at clubs, city parks, recreation centers, and sporting goods stores can be effective ways to promote business. People seeking tennis instruction frequently call high school and college physical education and athletic departments for information. Having contacts in those places can result in referrals.

The only equipment you need is a court, your racket, a basket of reasonably firm and fuzzy tennis balls, and enough tennis clothes to dress professionally. This does not mean that you must dress in whites only, but that you should be dressed neatly and comfortably. If you are going to teach professionally, you should dress accordingly. In addition to the equipment and clothes just mentioned, many clubs and city programs provide ball throwing machines for their instructors. These machines can be an effective teaching aid and should be used as an aid, not as a substitute teacher.

Once you are set up with people to teach, a place to teach, and equipment with which to teach, the next step is to plan what to teach. This obviously depends on factors such as who is to be taught, playing level, age, time available, and what the students want to learn. But there are some general principles which apply to almost any individual or group enrolled for instruction. Every lesson should be planned before you arrive at the courts. The planning should include what your goals for the day are, the teaching activities to be implemented, and a minute-by-minute timetable. Merely arriving at the courts ready to hit with your students is not enough. Try to get input from those being taught to help you decide about lesson content, but take the responsibility of planning what to do yourself. If you have several individuals or groups taking instruction separately but during the same time frame (weekly, for instance), it might be a good idea to keep a file card on each one. The card should contain information such as the name, address, and telephone number of the student, the lesson schedule, money paid or due, and a record of what has been done in previous lessons. Trying to keep track of two or three groups and several individuals without records is difficult.

Whether you are teaching individuals or groups, progression of learning is vital. Most teachers begin a series of lessons by teaching baseline fundamentals such as the ready position, forehand and backhand grips and strokes, the serve, and service return. As the students' skills improve, the teacher moves into halfcourt and forecourt skills such as approach shots, volleys, and the overhead smash. There is a temptation to tell a beginner or intermediate everything you know about the strokes. While the intent may be good, the student simply cannot assimilate that much information in a short period of time. If you and your students can concentrate on one component of a stroke at a time, all of the components will fall into place later. Overteaching tends to confuse and discourage many inexperienced players. If they are not very successful at first, they might conclude that there is just too much about tennis to learn and drop the sport. Teaching one concept at a time presents a problem. Repetition is essential, but it can be boring. It is your job to disguise the repetitive nature of learning strokes by designing enjoyable, variable, and constructive learning activities. Examples of drills are presented in the last section of this book.

Most people taking lessons want to learn something new every lesson and they want to feel that they have worked hard physically. Unless specific requests are made prior to a lesson by the students, the teaching sessions should be a combination of technical advice and stroke polishing and appropriate physical activity. Adults especially like to feel that they have gotten a workout when you are through with them. Give the people what they want. It is probably better to get to the technical part of a lesson first and to follow it with demanding drills and play. If the order is reversed, your students may be too tired to listen or learn.

If it is possible, try to arrange for some type of follow up to your lessons. Encourage your students to practice what they have learned by playing with others, hitting against a wall or a ball machine, or by going through serving drills alone. Be a match maker for students taking separate, private lessons. A group that takes lessons together is a natural for a weekly doubles match to complement the formal instruction.

Private (individual) lessons may be taught for one hour or half-hour periods. The pro who teaches half hour lessons is either very well or-

ganized and knowledgeable about the game or very business minded. A
teacher who works with a student for only thirty minutes must be very
good to keep his customers. There is no set number of individual lessons
a beginner should take, but one or two sessions a week should bring
results. There should be some time for the students to work on what has
been covered in the last lesson. Private lessons may last weeks, months,
or for indefinite periods of time, but after so many lessons the instructor
is probably repeating himself or correcting old mistakes rather than
introducing new information or techniques.

Quoting figures for the cost of private tennis lessons is risky because
of inflation and the supply and demand element. College players and
semi-professionals charge from five to ten dollars for an hour lesson,
and they are more likely to teach for an hour than a half hour. Club pros
get an average of five to fifteen dollars for a half hour session. Conscientious teaching pros can work out some kind of sliding pay scale for
younger players or those who cannot afford the high price of instruction.
Many instructors allow students to work for their lessons by shagging
balls, stringing rackets, or clerking in the pro shop. Payment for lessons
should be made by check for record keeping and tax purposes, and
should be made after a lesson or series of lessons. Prepayment can be a
problem in cases of bad weather, illness, or unexpected postponements.
Students should let you know in advance if they cannot be present for
a lesson so you can arrange your schedule accordingly.

Group lessons usually last an hour. The number of lessons per series
varies, but a one hour lesson once a week for six or eight weeks is average. Groups should have a minimum of four people and a maximum
of eight. Less than four will not be financially feasible for the teacher,
and more than eight is too many for effective instruction. Four, five, or
six people can be taught on one court if the instructor is well organized.
If seven or eight learners are in a group, two courts and an assistant
instructor should be used. Prices for group lessons may be one-third to
one-half as much as the cost for private lessons.

There are several abilities that the tennis teacher should possess.
First, he must be willing to do hard, physical work. Standing and moving
on the courts in all sorts of weather while constantly talking to students
is not an easy way to make a living. Most people do not understand that
even though tennis is recreation for them, it is an occupation for the
teaching pro. While that occupation can be rewarding in many ways,
it is not quite as glamorous as most people think. Second, the teacher
should be good at names—good enough to know every student by his
or her first name during the first lesson and to remember it the next
lesson. Believe it or not, there are professional tennis instructors who
still address some of their students as, "Hey, you!" during the fifth or

sixth week of instruction. That kind of behavior is not only rude, it is also bad business. The instructor should also be a good tosser and hitter. A good tosser can place the ball exactly where it should be placed and at the right speed for each student. For young beginners, tossing underhand may be appropriate for technical and psychological reasons. A good hitting teacher can keep the ball in play, hit it to the desired spot, and watch the student's movements rather than watching the ball. He must also be capable of carrying a hand full of balls while running about the court and hitting. This technique is terrible for the instructor's game because it requires a short backswing, little follow through, no opposite hand support, and no pace. Few top notch instructors can maintain their playing level while teaching heavy loads.

TEACHING PHYSICAL EDUCATION CLASSES

There is a wide range of competencies among the people now teaching tennis. The demand for instruction is so great, almost anyone who can play at the intermediate or advanced level will eventually be asked to teach some individual or group how to play the game. Although the demand for tennis teachers is encouraging, the quality of instruction is rather low. People who can play the game well cannot necessarily teach others how to play. While clubs, municipalities, and individuals are free to employ anyone they choose and can afford, schools should be as selective as possible in providing teachers who are not only tennis oriented, but educationally oriented.

The person reading this chapter has either already been selected or is interested in teaching tennis in a physical education program. If that decision has already been made, it would be useless to tell you what competencies you should possess to be qualified to teach tennis in schools. However, there are skills, teaching techniques, and information the tennis instructor should possess. If you do not have these competencies, it would be professionally advantageous to work toward certain goals in order to improve while you teach.

There are some great tennis teachers who have never had any formal training program to prepare them as instructors. Through experience and by using common sense they have reached high levels of competency. But for most people, there should be at least some tentative standards of preparation, and the following general guidelines are offered as suggestions to establish these standards:

1. The tennis instructor should have several years playing experience.

2. The tennis instructor should have competed in city, state, regional, or national tournaments.

3. The tennis instructor should have completed some formal program of tennis instruction (series of lessons, a tennis course, a clinic, etc.)

4. The instructor should have completed some formal educational program of methods in teaching tennis or physical education.

5. The instructor should have completed a course in human growth and development or psychology.

6. The instructor should have some experience in organizing and directing various forms of competition.

7. The instructor should be a member of some professional organization related to tennis, physical education, or education.

8. The instructor should subscribe to at least one professional publication related to tennis or physical education.

Preparing to Teach a Course

If you know you are going to teach a course, there are many areas of preparation to consider before the series of classes begins. The nature of your students—physical education majors, nonmajors, students required to take the course, students taking an elective course—has a lot to do with how you will prepare. Some of the decisions that have to be made may have already been determined by school or departmental policy, tradition, or unwritten guidelines of other teachers. If this is the case, all you have to do is check with your supervisor to learn what the policies are. If not, you should decide on the items below before you meet the first class. The intent here is not to suggest policies, but to alert you as to what must be planned.

1. Who will furnish tennis balls and rackets, how many will be needed, how should they be marked, and where will they be stored? Some schools provide all equipment for their students and others require the students to bring their own rackets and two or three marked balls. If the students bring their own balls, time will be needed at the end of each class to retrieve and sort out everyone's balls. Storage can be provided by the school or made the responsibility of the students.

2. Have the courts been cleared for use by your class? Check to see that there is no schedule conflict with other teachers, other departments, private groups, or varsity teams. Also check to see if the courts are in good playing condition.

3. How will students dress and what provisions are there for storage and cleaning of clothes and towels? The alternatives for dress are no special requirements, gym shorts and T-shirts, and school PE uniforms. As with equipment, storage can be the responsibility of the school or the students.

4. What are the objectives of the course? If not already established, they will vary with the nature of the students taking the course. If you are asked to write objectives, they will probably have to be written in behavioral terms (meaning in terms of student behavior, observable, and measurable). For example, "The learner will demonstrate proficiency in the serve by successfully serving seven of ten balls using the proper grip and a full swing motion."

5. Is there a course outline to follow? If not, an outline should be developed with a scope (content) and sequence (progression of learning activities) format. Suggestions for an outline are presented in this chapter.

6. What will students be assigned in addition to class activities? Written reports, magazine articles, participation in extraclass competition, attendance at tennis matches, unit plans, lesson plans, and field trips are possibilities, depending on the group taking the course.

7. How will the students be graded? Factors which may be considered are skill tests, written tests, written work assignments, attendance, improvement, and attitude. Examples of skill tests, written tests, and outside assignments are given in this chapter.

8. What is the policy on injuries? If a student is injured and cannot participate in the activities, there must be some policy established. Some schools give incompletes, others require the student to drop the course, others allow grading based on written work only, and some set a maximum grade which can be attained without full participation.

9. What is the policy on absences? Some programs build in an automatic penalty for missing classes. In others, as long as work is successfully completed, attendance is not a factor in grading. A plan for making up work missed must also be devised.

10. How will the class be organized? A class routine will be necessary for checking attendance, arranging for lectures or demonstrations, and learning activities. Many instructors assign students to permanent groups for drills. Groups of four or less per court is ideal; six in a group is crowded, but manageable; and more than six is undesirable.

11. How will the class be taught on bad weather days? Make sure there is some place for your class to meet, and prepare some classroom presentations in advance.

Teaching the Course

Lengths of tennis courses vary with the schools. Some meet daily for an entire semester. Others meet two or three times a week. Class periods range from forty minutes to two hours. Required physical education tennis courses frequently consist of on the court work only. Classes for future teachers usually combine playing time and classroom instruction. Regardless of the length of the class period or course, the most important factors are the content and the sequence of progression of learning activities. Here is an outline for a tennis class of nonmajors which will meet thirty times (five days a week for six weeks). Each class period will last sixty minutes with approximately forty to forty-five minutes of actual court time.

1st Day   Introduction to course
Format and instructions on procedures
Assign students a tennis article to read

2nd Day   Explain and demonstrate ready position, forehand grip and stroke
Large group drills followed by partner or small group drills

3rd Day   Review fundamentals of forehand
Demonstrate how to drop ball and put it into play
Repeat forehand drills

4th Day   Explain and demonstrate backhand grip and stroke
Class and small group drills

5th Day   Review fundamentals of backhand
Repeat drills

6th Day   Classroom lesson on rules, equipment, and terms
Discussion of articles; assign second article
Questions and answers

7th Day   Explain and demonstrate punch and/or full swing serve
Class and group drills

8th Day   Review fundamentals of serve
Repeat serving drills

9th Day   Explain and demonstrate forehand and backhand volley
Partner or small group drills

10th Day   Review fundamentals of volley
Drills for the volley

11th Day	Explain and demonstrate overhead smash Drills for the smash Repeat drills for other strokes or free play
12th Day	Classroom lesson on singles and doubles strategy Questions and answers
13th Day	Singles or doubles play
14th Day	Singles or doubles play
15th Day	Explain and demonstrate lob and drop shot Drills

16th Day	Drills for groundstrokes Singles or doubles play
17th Day	Drills for the serve Combination drills
18th Day	Drills for the net game Singles or doubles play
19th Day	Singles or doubles competition (Tournament)
20th Day	Singles or doubles competition

21st Day	Singles or doubles competition
22nd Day	Singles or doubles competition
23rd Day	Classroom lesson; discussion of second reading assignment Review for written test
24th Day	Practice for skill tests
25th Day	Practice for skill tests

26th Day	Skill tests; play for those not taking tests today
27th Day	Skill tests; play
28th Day	Skill tests; play
29th Day	Skill tests; play
30th Day	Written final exam

Giving Skill Tests

The teacher who designs or administers skill tests for physical education activity courses will always be faced with the problem of whether to consider improvement as a factor in the final grade. Pretests and posttests should be considered as a measurement technique, but both have negative aspects. The student who comes into your class never having played tennis is more likely to show progress than the person who has some playing experience. It makes sense to reward the beginner for improvement, but the intermediate or advanced player should not be penalized for something over which he has little control.

A second problem is whether to grade on accuracy, form, or a combination of the two. Some of the standardized tennis tests award grades on accuracy. For example, a student can punch the ball on the serve using a western grip and probably score high on accuracy. A second student may attempt the full swing serve using good form, but hit fewer shots into the target area. A combination of form and accuracy seems to be the most equitable alternative, but it leaves part of the grading to a subjective evaluation by the teacher. If you are not ready to assume that responsibility, it might be better to grade objectively and solely on the placement of shots.

The third problem to be solved in giving skill tests involves which skills to test. The level of competence among the students should be the determining factor in your selection. For beginning players, the following aspects of the game should be sufficient to establish a fair skill grade:

1. Demonstration of the ready position
2. Demonstration of proper grips
3. Put ball into play by dropping and hitting
4. Return hit or thrown balls with forehand stroke
5. Return hit or thrown balls with backhand stroke
6. Serve—punch or full swing
7. Return hit or thrown balls with forehand volley
8. Return hit or thrown balls with backhand volley
9. Return hit or thrown balls with overhead smash
10. Overall playing ability

Intermediate or advanced players should be able to perform the same skills at a higher level of competence as well as these:

11. Demonstration of proper footwork for each stroke
12. Demonstration of variety of serves
13. Demonstration of the lob
14. Demonstration of the drop shot
15. Demonstration of the half volley

Often there is not sufficient time to test each student on all skills. In that case, certain skills should be selected as indicators of overall ability. The number of attempts allowed each student per stroke should not be less than five and not more than ten (because of time considerations). Each student should be allowed to practice a few shots before beginning a skill test. In addition to individual stroke skills, some provision should be made for the students to hit against another player who can keep the ball in play or against the instructor. The overall hitting ability should be taken into account as part of that player's skill grade. A student may do poorly on individual shots attempted out of a game context, but do quite well by keeping the ball in play and using a variety of shots while moving. The overall hitting score should carry more weight than the scores achieved on separate strokes. That score is not only more important, but it also gives the instructor the opportunity to use his judgment in determining the final skill grade.

A skill test form is shown on the next page. The students have been tested on eight variables valued from one to five points. One was the lowest a student could score; five was the highest. Grading was based on a combination of form and accuracy. The overall hitting grade was scored from one to ten. The final skill grade may be determined by a predetermined number of points necessary to achieve an "A," "B," "C," "D," or "F," or the scores may be curved to allow for the group's skill level. In this example, the scores were curved.

Giving Written Tests

The most commonly used items on written tests are true-false, multiple choice, identification, discussion, matching, fill-in-the-blank, and listing. Matching items are not very demanding and allow for guessing by the process of elimination. Fill-in-the-blank questions are too structured and give no opportunity for original responses. Listing items requires memorization, which is a rather superficial way to learn. The other types of written tests should be more reliable and valid, but they also have advantages and disadvantages. True-false tests can be an effective method of evaluation, but care must be taken to use words familiar to the student and to structure statements so that they will not appear vague or ambiguous to the students. Properly constructed true-false tests should have a majority of true statements. People tend to remember as fact what they read, whether it is true or not. Multiple choice tests should have at least three items from which to choose and not more than five. Identification of terms may constitute part of a test, but an entire test of identification items again requires too much memory work. Discussion items are the best way to ascertain what a student knows, but the time required for grading this type of test may be prohibitive. A written test should include a maximum of three different

Skill Test Form

NAME	Serve	Forehand	Backhand	Forehand Volley	Backhand Volley	Overhead Smash	General Play	Total Score	Skill Grade
Hornsby	3	3	2	4	1	3	6	22	C
Roberts	4	5	4	4	3	5	8	33	A
Anderson	3	3	4	3	4	3	6	26	B-
Stedman	2	3	2	4	4	2	5	22	C
Pilgreen	3	4	3	4	3	3	7	27	B
Pendas	5	5	4	3	4	5	8	34	A
Leis	3	3	3	2	3	4	5	23	C
Chapman	4	4	5	3	3	5	9	33	A-
Armand	4	4	3	3	4	2	8	28	B
Cutshaw	2	2	3	1	1	2	3	14	D
Cornwell	3	3	3	3	2	4	5	23	C
Bono	2	3	2	3	3	2	6	21	C
Stewart	1	3	3	4	3	3	7	24	C+
Ciszek	5	5	5	5	4	4	9	37	A
Lewis	2	1	1	2	2	3	4	15	D
Layman	4	4	3	2	3	2	6	24	C+
Pumpelly	4	4	4	4	2	3	7	28	B
Kloor	5	4	5	4	3	3	5	29	B
Fruge	5	4	3	2	3	2	5	24	C+
Bohnke	3	3	2	2	4	1	5	20	C
Curry	4	5	2	4	3	3	6	27	B

Figure 3-1.

kinds of questions. Anything beyond this becomes more of an obstacle course exercise than a measure of what has been learned. On the following pages are sample true-false, multiple choice, identification, and discussion items. These questions are not presented as a test but as possible questions from which a teacher may choose.

True or False:

T 1. When the score is 30–15, the server is winning the game.

T 2. Balls that land on lines are in play.

F 3. It is illegal to serve with an underhand motion.

T 4. A let serve is repeated.

T 5. A player may not reach over the net to strike a ball.

F 6. The backswing used to hit a volley is the same used to hit a groundstroke.

F 7. Clay courts are faster than concrete courts.

T 8. A doubles team may change the order of serve at the beginning of a new set.

T 9. Davis Cup play involves international competition for men.

T 10. The governing body for amateur tennis in the U. S. is the United States Tennis Association.

F 11. The player about to receive a serve may purposely attempt to distract the server.

T 12. A player must win at least eight games and be ahead by at least two games to win a pro set.

F 13. The server must have at least one foot in contact with the ground when the ball is served.

T 14. The grips for the backhand and advanced serve are similar.

T 15. The arm should be fully extended at the point of contact on the serve.

F 16. The lob should only be used as a defensive tactic.

T 17. A shot with backspin is called a chop.

F 18. A short stroke with a wrist snap is recommended for groundstrokes.

T 19. A maximum of one minute is allowed for players to change ends of the court after an odd number of games.

T 20. In some instances, the player who wins the toss or racket spin should choose a side rather than first serve.

T 21. A foot fault should be called when a player walks or runs as part of the service delivery.

T 22. A shot is good if it is returned outside the net post and lands in the proper court.

T 23. In a nine point tie-breaker, the player due to serve the next game with the score 6–6 serves the first two points.

T   24. Playing an Australian doubles formation, the server and his partner line up on the same side of the court.

T   25. If other variables are equal, a flat serve will have more velocity
than a twist serve.

F   26. Passing shots should be hit as high over the net as possible.

F   27. Professionals and amateurs are not allowed to compete in the
same tournaments in this country.

T   28. A service toss may be repeated if the ball is not hit.

F   29. In hitting a backhand, the ball should be struck at a point even
with the center of the body.

T   30. When both opponents are at the net in doubles, the best place
to hit is low and down the middle.

T   31. In doubles play, lefthanders are usually more effective returning
a serve from the left side of the court.

F   32. The net is the same height in the middle as at the sideline.

T   33. A player attempting a topspin shot can hit the ball higher over
the net than with other shots.

T   34. Put-away overhead smashes should not be attempted from a
position behind the baseline.

T   35. Drop shots should not be attempted when the wind is at a
player's back.

T   36. In tournament competition, players should be allowed at least
fifteen minutes between matches.

T   37. Most points are decided by errors rather than by winners.

F   38. The height of the player is not a factor in executing a serve.

T   39. Most approach shots should be hit down the line.

T   40. The Wightman Cup is awarded to the winner of a dual match
between women of the United States and England.

F   41. Gut strings are water resistant.

T   42. Metal rackets generally allow a player to hit with more force
than wooden rackets do.

T   43. Hard court surfaces are easier to maintain than soft surfaces.

F   44. The server's partner in doubles should stand in the alley.

T   45. The server's motion in tennis is similar to the throwing motion
in baseball.

T   46. In singles, keeping the ball deep is more important than hitting
shots that barely clear the net.

T   47. Most groundstrokes should be hit crosscourt.

T 48. Backhand shots are more likely to be hit with backspin than forehand shots.

T 49. Lobs should be directed to an opponent's backhand.

F 50. The racket should be brought back on the backswing just as the ball bounces in front of the hitter.

Multiple Choice

1. Which of the following tournaments is considered to be the most prestigious in the world?
   (1) U. S. Open, (2) French Open, (3) **Wimbledon,** (4) World Team Tennis Championships.

2. You are serving and the score is 30–40. Your opponent wins the next point. The score is now
   (1) **game,** (2) 30–45, (3) deuce, (4) ad out.

3. What is the minimum number of points possible in a game?
   (1) 3, (2) **4,** (3) 5, (4) 6.

4. What is the maximum number of sets played in women's competition?
   (1) one set, (2) one pro set, (3) **two out of three sets,** (4) three out of five sets.

5. Where is the best place to wait for the ball during singles play?
   (1) center of the court, (2) **middle of the baseline,** (3) on the service line, (4) anywhere in the backcourt.

6. Which of these scores would be called deuce?
   (1) each player has two points, (2) each player has the same number of points, (3) **each player has three points,** (4) 30–30.

7. In doubles, shots hit down the middle should be taken
   (1) **by the player with the forehand shot,** (2) by the player closest to the net, (3) by the player with the backhand shot, (4) by the last player to hit the ball on the previous shot.

8. Players must change ends of the court after every
   (1) point, (2) game, (3) set, (4) **odd game.**

9. The height of the net at the center of the court is
   (1) 2½ feet, (2) **3 feet,** (3) 3½ feet, (4) none of these.

10. The serve should be hit with the ball
    (1) **in front of the body,** (2) directly over the server's head, (3) slightly behind the head, (4) to the left of the server's head.

11. A shot hit with topspin will
    (1) **bounce higher than usual,** (2) lower than usual, (3) have the same bounce as any other shot, (4) bounce to the left of the opponent.

12. A closed stance may indicate that the hitter is going to hit (1) **straight ahead,** (2) crosscourt, (3) a lob, (4) a slice.

13. Which is the least effective grip for hitting a backhand shot?
    (1) Eastern, (2) **Western,** (3) Continental, (4) handshake.

14. In doubles, the receiver's partner should stand
    (1) just in front of the baseline, (2) two steps from the net, (3) **on the service line,** (4) in the alley.

15. In doubles, when the ball is lobbed over the net player's head, he should
    (1) stay where he is, (2) **cross to the other side of the court,** (3) try to beat his partner to the ball, (4) move to the center of the court.

16. Which shot would be the best to use against a short lob?
    (1) drop shot, (2) **smash,** (3) lob, (4) topspin backhand.

17. If a ball rolls onto the court during a rally, the point
    (1) should be continued, (2) is given to the player on whose side the ball is rolling, (3) **should be replayed,** (4) is awarded to the player on the other side of the court.

18. The United States Open Tennis Championships are played in
    (1) Los Angeles, (2) **Forest Hills, New York,** (3) Dallas, (4) Miami.

19. The receiving formation of a doubles team
    (1) **may be changed at the end of a set,** (2) may not be changed after the match has begun, (3) may be changed at any time during the match, (4) is not restricted by any rule.

20. The most popular type of tennis tournament is the
    (1) double elimination, (2) **single elimination,** (3) round robin, (4) ladder.

21. The best grip to use in hitting the volley is the
    (1) **Continental,** (2) Western, (3) Eastern, (4) modified Eastern.

22. If a ball is touched by a player who is standing behind the baseline before it bounces,
    (1) **he loses the point,** (2) he wins the point, (3) the point is replayed, (4) the umpire may rule for either player.

23. In the last point of a nine point tie-breaker,
    (1) the players flip to determine the court to be served from, (2) the server decides on which court to serve from, (3) **the receiver decides on which court he prefers to receive,** (4) the umpire decides on which court to be served from.

24. A player who has been drawn off to one side of the court behind the baseline should attempt which shot?
    (1) **a lob,** (2) a drop shot, (3) a smash, (4) a crosscourt groundstroke.

25. Which of the following strokes will involve movement of the wrist?
    (1) forehand, (2) backhand, (3) volley, (4) **smash.**

Definition or Identification of Terms

U.S.T.A.	baseline	flat
I.L.T.F.	service line	Australian doubles
slice	alley	tie breaker
chop	advantage	straight sets
pace	foot fault	round robin
push	World Team Tennis	ladder tournament
seed	pivot	pyramid tournament
gut	racket head	love
deuce	racket throat	rally
American twist	topspin	volley
Continental	approach shot	poach
half volley	passing shot	rush
bye	ace	double elimination
VASSS	stop volley	hook
chip	closed stance	open stance
default	semi-finals	quarter-finals
Wimbledon	W.C.T.	Davis Cup
Bill Tilden	Billie Jean King	Rod Laver
Pancho Gonzales	Walter Wingfield	Althea Gibson

Discussion Questions:

1. Explain the scoring system in tennis.
2. Explain the nine point tie-breaker system.
3. Diagram and discuss the positions for advanced doubles.
4. Name and explain the three basic tennis grips.
5. Discuss the advantages and disadvantages of metal and wooden rackets.

6. Name and discuss the advantages and disadvantages of the various kinds of racket strings.

7. Name and discuss the advantages and disadvantages of the various kinds of court surfaces.

8. Trace the history of tennis from the 1800s to the present.

9. Give some examples of basic singles strategy.

10. Give some examples of basic doubles strategy.

11. Discuss the possibilities for positioning the different combinations of righthanded and lefthanded players in doubles.

12. Explain how a round robin tournament is drawn up and conducted.

13. Explain the procedure for seeding players in a tournament.

14. Compare tennis to golf, bowling, swimming, and handball in terms of endurance, strength, balance, speed, flexibility, and quickness.

15. Outline and discuss the organizational structure of the United States Tennis Association.

Assigning Work for Future Teachers

Physical education majors, minors, and others who will eventually teach tennis to groups of people should develop their own resource units for future use. Although books such as this one are a type of teaching unit, students will be more likely to use something they have worked out for themselves. They certainly will be more familiar with the material they decide to include in a unit than with the information in a book. Some college teachers require their students to develop a unit plan and others ask their students to prepare a series of daily lesson plans. Below are content suggestions for unit and lesson plans.

Unit Plan Outline:

    I. Introduction
       A. History
       B. Values
   II. Unit Objectives
       A. General objectives or goals
       B. Specific objectives
          1. Written in terms of the learner
          2. Related to general objectives
          3. What is to be accomplished by each individual

 III. Development of the Activity
  A. Skills or techniques to be taught
  B. Key teaching points
  C. Lead-up games or special activities
  D. Tennis-related information (principles, rules, strategy, etiquette, etc.)
 IV. Class Organization
  A. Division of students into groups
  B. Assignment to teaching stations
 V. Equipment
 VI. Health and Safety Precautions
  A. Safety rules
  B. Physical examinations
 VII. Motivational Devices
  A. Audio-visual aids
  B. Tournaments
  C. Field trips
  D. Special events
 VIII. Evaluation and Measurement
  A. Skill tests
  B. Written tests
  C. Assignments
 IX. Block Plan
  A. Time table of lesson plans
  B. Progression of learning activities
 X. References
  A. Books
  B. Periodicals
  C. Miscellaneous material

Daily Lesson Plan Outline:

 I. Objectives (written in behavioral terms)
 II. Equipment (items necessary to conduct the class)
 III. Time Allotment (how many minutes for each class segment)
 IV. New Material (outline of lecture notes, if any)
 V. Activities (explanation and diagram of learning activities)
 VI. Evaluation (self-evaluation or notes on lesson taught)
 VII. References (sources of information used in this lesson)

4 Coaching The Sport

COACHING IN HIGH SCHOOL

Although tennis is more popular now than ever before, the supply of qualified coaches remains limited. Many high school and even college coaches have little or no background in the sport. Many faculty members are literally stuck with the job. The tennis coach may be an assistant football coach who does not have a spring assignment, a first year science teacher, anybody who has mentioned that he or she likes tennis, or someone else equally unqualified. If you consider yourself reasonably experienced and qualified as a high school coach, this chapter is not for you. If you can identify with the people just described, there may be information in this section that will be helpful to you as a learning tennis coach.

The instant coach can do one of two things about coaching a team. He can go through the motions by throwing out the tennis balls at practice and serving as a chaperone or sponsor on trips. Or the coach without a strong tennis background can take the job seriously and attempt to become worthy of the new title.

Although it is almost impossible for the inexperienced coach to actually teach someone to play tennis, he can become a relatively adequate coach. Coaching and teaching are two different matters. Coaches can concentrate on recruiting players, making schedules, preparing the team for competition through well organized practices, conducting matches, and promoting the tennis program among players, students, faculty members, and the public.

Tennis teachers must be able to show young players how to hold the racket, how to swing it, how to hit the ball, how to move their feet, and later on, how to win. Although the coach without a tennis background may learn enough about stroke production to do some teaching later in his career, it is too much to expect him to be both a coach and a teacher at the beginning.

An inexperienced coach can do some homework before assuming his duties. National, regional, state, and local tennis organizations, sporting goods companies, colleges and universities, and club professionals promote interest in the game by conducting clinics for players and coaches. Since there is no set schedule for most of these clinics, you have to watch the newspapers and professional magazines for information about clinics in your area.

Coaches can also increase their knowledge of the game by reading tennis literature. There are many tennis magazines and books containing instructional information for players, teachers, and coaches. Specific information about ways to increase your knowledge of tennis is included in Chapter 5 in a section entitled, "Developing Professionally."

Recruiting

When school starts in August or September, the coach must begin looking for the best athletes available for the team. Many coaches have a team meeting sometime during the fall semester. An announcement on the public address system, in the school paper, and on campus bulletin boards inviting those interested in playing varsity tennis to attend that meeting will usually attract enough players to get started. The core of your team will be those students who played on last year's squad. In addition to that group there may be a few transfer students, some players up from middle school or junior high school, and a few strays. Ask those who attend the first meeting if there are others they know who might be interested in playing. There will always be a few students who were either absent the day of the meeting, who did not know about the meeting, or who were not sure enough about their ability to try out for the team. Try to add two or three athletes who have proved themselves in other sports. You may not win a state championship with players who have played tennis for only two years, but a good athlete can improve enough in a season or two to give your team depth at the lower positions.

From a purely coaching standpoint, try to avoid the nonathlete who is not good enough to participate in any other sport. The curse of all minor sports is having to take in rejects from football, basketball, and baseball. From an educational point of view, take in as many bodies as you can while considering the time, courts, and supplies available. You may find a sleeper; if not, you can always direct the less gifted student to intramurals and summer tennis programs.

At the first team meeting, get as much information about your recruits as possible. Find out their names, ages, addresses, classes, schedules, playing experience, and anything else that will help you get to know them. If you plan to have a fall program, the meeting can be used to tell your players about what they will be doing in the coming weeks. You can also use this session to distribute medical forms, eligibility statements, and locks, and to talk about your policies regarding practices, equipment, and training rules. If you will not begin practice until the spring semester, get the information needed, let the players know how and when to get in touch with you, and announce the time and place for the next team meeting.

Ordering Supplies

Before you can do anything about buying supplies and equipment for your team, you have to check with the principal or athletic director to find out how much money is available and where the money will come from. Expect the worst when you go in to get this information. Tennis budgets are traditionally small. Do not be surprised if you are told that your money must come from self-generated funds earned in programs sales, car washes, concessions, or other rather unglamorous projects. It might be appropriate to complain about the amount of money allotted to tennis and to inquire about the sources of funds for other interscholastic athletics. Since you are a relatively new coach, your complaints probably will not get any immediate results, but you can start wearing down the establishment early. Once you have established yourself as a responsible coach and the program has earned some respectability, you will be in a better position to ask for a bigger tennis budget.

With the money available to tennis, you must then decide on a priority list of items in terms of what you need and what you can afford. The first item on most lists will be tennis balls. It is difficult to advise you on how many balls you will need because that will depend on how many players you have, how many matches at home your team will play, and how many months your fall and/or spring practices will run. It may be best to schedule your matches first, then determine the number of balls needed for home matches. With that number as a base figure and counting on match balls for practice sessions for two or three days following a match, you can begin to get an idea of how many balls to order. If you are still not sure, order a few dozen to get started, and place a second order when a pattern of use has developed. Solicit bids or at least compare prices before making a decision on which balls to purchase.

In addition to providing tennis balls, you will also have to consider racket restringing jobs, clothes and tennis shoes, and money for out of town matches and tournaments. Having rackets restrung can deplete a budget rapidly. A few high schools have enough money to pay for all restringing jobs, some schools allow one or two per varsity player, and others make their players pay for their own work. Here are four suggestions that may help you save money on racket strings: (1) Learn to string rackets or at least how to patch strings yourself. Not all breaks require a completely new set of strings. (2) Encourage your school to purchase a stringing machine so that players can string their own rackets. The initial investment for a machine could range from seventy-five to five hundred dollars, but the long range savings would be even more substantial. (3) Use racket string that is worthy of competition, but less expensive than gut. There are several kinds of nylon string that are relatively inexpensive and more than adequate for the average high school player. (4) Buy racket string in large quantities directly from the manufacturer instead of having to buy thirty-three feet of material in separate quantities for each stringing job done at a pro shop or sporting goods store.

The tennis clothes and shoes problem can also be sticky, but most schools provide shirts or blouses with the school emblem and perhaps one pair of shoes for each team member. The players have to buy everything else. Items such as socks and supporters may be available from supplies purchased for other school teams.

Finally, you will have to allocate some money for travel expenses such as gasoline, meals, and housing. It is not uncommon for tennis players in high school to be transported by parents, to buy meals with their own money, and to spend the night in homes of friends or host team players. This is not the way the football team travels, but you were told to expect the worst when it comes to tennis budgets. If you have the money available, take your team first class. You need no advice on how to do that.

Scheduling

Try to avoid making a schedule before you have had a chance to see your team practice for a while. Your schedule should be based on your team's ability. It is important that you allow your team the opportunity to be successful. Playing against rugged competition on the theory that your squad's game will improve is advisable, but only to a certain point. There are psychological factors involved in playing tennis, and players have to win their share of matches to have a winning attitude. At times, winning may be more important than rugged competition. At the end of a season, you and your team will be judged on how many matches you won and lost more than on who you played.

Factors such as money, the weather, available competition, the number of school courts, and league rules will have to be considered in determining how many matches or tournaments to schedule. In some states, most competition consists of dual matches between schools during the regular season, followed by district and state tournaments late in the spring. If the dual match format is used where you coach, try to arrange enough matches to keep interest high, but not so many that students have to miss many classes or spend all their time playing rather than practicing. At the high school level, players' games are still in a developmental stage and practicing is probably more important than constant formal competition. A schedule of at least one match a week and not more than two matches should be sufficient for a balance between playing and practicing.

In other states, the pattern of competition is for each school in an area to host a single elimination tournament once during the season. In a heavily populated area, this kind of arrangement usually means your team could play a tournament every weekend. Single elimination tournaments are the backbone of tennis, but an overemphasis on this form of competition at the interscholastic level reduces the emphasis on having a well balanced group of players on one team. Playing only weekend tournaments, the weaker players are fortunate if they get to participate at all when the number of entrants is limited. When they do play, they are likely to lose and to be eliminated after the first round. The team that has one or two outstanding players or doubles combinations is likely to do well while the better balanced team may lose in the early rounds.

You may not have a choice about the form of competition in your district or league, but if the single elimination format is predominant, try to provide some type of intrasquad, dual match, or junior varsity program for the players who rank fourth, fifth, sixth, or lower on your team.

Conducting Practice Sessions

An entire section of Chapter 4 is devoted to organizing practices, but there are some general guidelines which seem especially appropriate for the inexperienced coach. With a little preparation you can conduct a structured, purposeful practice session. Every player should spend some time almost every day working on fundamentals. All players need practice grooving their strokes for down-the-line shots, crosscourt groundstrokes, volleys, serves, and overhead smashes. This kind of practice and a simple serve, rush, and volley drill can be administered by any coach.

Do not let your players hit without a purpose or merely play matches in practice. Just hitting or playing can reinforce bad habits

Experienced players on your team can help you plan practices. Do not be embarrassed to ask your best players what they want to work on during a session. Be careful about letting them spend too much time playing sets, and avoid intense competition the day before a match or tournament.

Whatever you do in practice, do not apologize for your lack of technical knowledge. Your players know how much you know about tennis, so there is no reason to emphasize a negative point. You can gain your players' respect by taking your job seriously, by doing the best you can, and by not attempting to hide anything from them. By being enthusiastic as well as professional, you can overcome a multitude of technical deficiencies. You do not have to be a tennis nut, but you can be proud of your position and let your players know that you take pride in their accomplishments.

Conducting Dual Matches

You may be able to avoid conducting a single elimination tournament until you have gained some experience, but you will probably have to know how to conduct dual matches the first year. Matches between two schools involving a set number of singles and doubles are easy to arrange and conduct if you are willing to give attention to details. When you are arranging the schedule for the coming season, you will have already exchanged letters with other coaches to establish dates, times, places, and type of competition (pro sets, two out of three sets, number of matches to be played, etc.). A few days before each match, call or write the opposing coach to reconfirm the date and time and to give him information about dressing facilities. The day before the match, let your players know who will be playing, what their respective positions will be, and what time they should be at the courts.

On the day of the match, you or someone you designate should be responsible for getting the following supplies to the courts: enough new tennis balls for each match to be played, towels, scoreboards, a first aid kit, water containers, and score sheets if they are to be used.

It is appropriate for you and your players to introduce yourselves to the visiting team and for you to introduce all players to the spectators. See that new balls are given to each pair of singles participants and give them instructions about special ground rules, tie-breakers, third set balls, and to whom to report scores and return the balls after the match. Once the match begins, there is nothing you can do except try to keep up with all the matches simultaneously and to see that the crowd does not interfere with play. Some conferences allow coaches to talk to their players when they change ends of the court, but others do not. Find out what is proper in your area. You should roam throughout the match and try to watch each of your players for part of his match. Your attention will give you more insight into each player's game and it will be encouraging to your team members to know that you are keeping up with their progress. This is especially true for the players in lower line-up positions. There is nothing wrong with asking the score as long as you ask at a time when play or concentration on the next point is not interfered with. Let your players know before the match that you will be asking for their scores periodically.

Once the singles matches have been completed, you or the umpire should record each score. Try to speak to your players privately after a match. If they win, congratulate them. If they lose, be positive, but ask them how the match went. After a reasonable rest period, get the doubles matches started by calling for the players by their names. Make sure that your players do not wander off while waiting for doubles competition to begin. When the doubles matches have been played, again record the scores and collect the used balls. Unless your players have to be somewhere else, ask them to stay at the courts until all matches have been completed. The team is playing a match and each player should remain to watch his teammates compete. You may want to have a team meeting after the match. Before leaving, make sure that the visiting team has a place to shower and dress.[1]

BUILDING A COLLEGE TEAM

In college tennis, probably more than any other sport, it is possible to go from a very weak program or no program at all to one of conference championship calibre in one year. This rags to riches possibility exists because only five or six athletes are needed to make up a team, because there are very few college coaches who know enough or care enough to do selective recruiting, and because tennis ability in a player shows up early and is rather predictable.

It is not unusual for a number one player to win the conference championship in his first year, and to continue winning it during his college career. Not only do tennis players either have it or not have it by the time they are eighteen or nineteen years old, the best players usually win. This means that the role of the coach as a teacher in tennis

[1]Jim Brown, "Coaching Without a Background," *Scholastic Coach*, 40, no. 6 (February, 1971) 42.

is less important at the college level than in other sports. The outstanding tennis player is seldom developed into championship material by a college coach, nor is he likely to be overcoached (as probably happens in some other sports) to the point of not playing up to his potential.

While overnight success is possible at the college level, it is not automatic or easy. A college or university must have a person willing to put in the time and effort necessary to develop the program. The school must also have the money to invest in scholarships and a reasonable budget in order to turn a program around in one year.

While it is advantageous if the coach knows something about playing tennis, it is not absolutely essential. The strength of a college tennis coach lies in recruiting, promoting, organizing, budgeting, handling players, and putting in time with the players, not in teaching people how to play the game. The college coach who has to teach tennis to his players is going to lose. The coach who says he is rebuilding is hoping for a miracle.

Assuming that there is someone on the faculty or staff who has the time and interest to coach tennis, the next ingredient is scholarships. A school cannot expect to field a good team consistently without at least five full scholarships. There may be exceptions to this in urban areas where high school and summer programs are strong and many players are available, but a champion tennis player deserves and will be offered a full scholarship somewhere. After a winning tradition has been established, it may be possible to get quality players for less than full financial support. Without the tennis reputation and without enough full scholarships, a college's goals in terms of winning and losing should be limited.

Recruiting

Once the scholarship issue has been decided, the coach has to use his grants-in-aid very wisely. In football, some universities carry as many as a hundred players on scholarships. If mistakes are made in selecting a few players, it is not likely to show up in the win-loss column. In tennis, there are five or six players on a team. No freshman team. No junior varsity. The college tennis coach is going to win or lose with the five or six players he recruits. Recruiting is not just an important factor in winning, it is the determining factor. Because recruiting is so vital to the eventual success or failure of a college program, special attention will be given to the problem here.

There are four places to look for college tennis recruits: in high schools, in junior colleges, in other countries, and in the armed services. For most coaches, players are available in the order just listed and will be considered in that order.

Each year thousands of high school players graduate and would like to attend colleges on scholarships, but only a fraction of that number has enough talent to be considered college material. In order to select the ones who can contribute to your program, you should begin attending local and regional tournaments to spot high school upperclassmen who consistently advance to the quarterfinals, semifinals, and finals. It is flattering and motivating for a high school athlete to know that he is being watched by a professional talent scout, which is what you are to him.

If everything else is equal, the players to watch are the ones who win often and the ones who have good strokes. Unfortunately, everything else is not usually equal. Too often in tennis and in other sports, the super player with all the shots is also the one who has been spoiled by his parents, his coach, and the fans. The good competitor with a winning attitude, but with less than perfect form, may be as valuable to you as the world class player. Good college teams need depth as much as they do an outstanding number one player.

From a public relations standpoint, it is a good idea to know as many high school players as possible, but you should set your sights on a few athletes and give them the most attention. It is better to over-recruit without committing yourself to more scholarships than you have than to gamble on one player, only to lose him to another school. Business cards and brochures describing your program are inexpensive and easy to distribute to anyone who will take one.

Once you have selected the few players who could help you, it is important to keep in touch with them from the time you meet them until they enter your college. Athletes like to see their names in print, and sending them newspaper clippings about your team helps the potential recruit identify with your school. Send them anything you have to keep them interested in the program—newspapers, the college catalogue, brochures, pictures, and personal letters. Even sending a high school player a birthday card signed by your players might help.

If you have a prospect interested in attending your college, talk tennis with him, but talk school, discipline, academic standards, and scholarship benefits with his parents. If your program is already strong, approach the prospect on the basis of becoming part of a winning team, and let him know that his game will improve by practicing with your players. If your program is weak, tell him you want to build a solid program by signing players of his ability. He will like the idea of playing a high position as a freshman, even though that might not be good for him. Do your homework before talking to the player or his parents. Try to learn what his interests are and which academic program he will enter. A major university will sell itself. If you coach at a smaller institution, emphasize points such as friendly atmosphere, good teacher-student ratio, and the personal attention each student gets. Do not hesitate to sell yourself as a coach, family man, or guardian. If you can convince Mom and Dad that you are going to take care of their boy, the size of your school will not be as important a factor.

Using players already on your squad can also be an effective recruiting technique. When a high school player visits your campus, let him spend part of the time visiting with your players. If your program is a good one, your players will sell it for you.

Recruiting in junior college presents some new problems, but can be easier than dealing with high school boys in some respects. Junior college transfer students are more mature, have better ideas about their academic goals, and ask more specific questions. They are great for plugging the gap when you have been hit hard by graduation, but you have to recruit every two years instead of four. These men have played for another coach and will be comparing you to him. Their tennis game is probably as developed as it is going to be, so you cannot afford to make a mistake in judging their ability. If a high school recruit is weaker than you expected, he has four years to improve. A junior college transfer has half as much time. Be careful about checking the junior college student's grades. Some students attend two-year-schools because they are not strong enough to make it at a four-year-school.

The quickest way to turn a losing program into a winning one is to recruit foreign players. The amount of work involved in finding and signing them is staggering, but worth the trouble. If you have friends in other countries, ask them to help you find prospects. The best selling point is an American education. If you do not have overseas contacts, write to national tennis associations about your program and let them know you have scholarships available.

Allow yourself more time in recruiting foreign players than with Americans. If your college belongs to the National Collegiate Athletic Association, your prospects may have to take special tests. Each institution will have special entrance requirements for foreign students. All correspondence should be conducted by air mail in order to minimize time problems.

The fourth source of tennis prospects is the armed forces. There is not a great supply of players in the military who will be looking for scholarships, but there are enough to justify writing a few letters. Find out who is available by writing to athletic directors at military bases. The veteran will be older and probably more serious about getting an education. However, he may have attended another college previously and will have to complete 24 semester hours at your school before becoming eligible for intercollegiate competition.

Once players begin to respond to your feelers, it may be difficult to decide on who should be offered the scholarships. Tennis players have a way of making themselves look great on paper. If a coach is knowledgeable about the game, he does not need advice on who to select. If he is not, all he can do is analyze a player's record, watch him play, if possible, look at his grades and references, and go to someone to get a technical evaluation of the recruit's ability. Every coach is going to be disappointed by recruiting a player who does not measure up to his clippings, so do not expect to be 100 percent successful the first year.[2]

Scheduling

The coach should begin arranging the spring schedule early during the fall semester. A slate of fifteen to twenty dual matches and two or three tournaments is a full, if not heavy, schedule. When teams play more than this, the players have trouble keeping up with academic work. If you have inherited a losing program, it is important to schedule some early matches that you can reasonably expect to win. Early season success helps your players get their games in shape before meeting tougher opponents, makes them more confident, and establishes a winning image of your program at school and in the community.

Ordering Supplies

Early during the fall semester is also the time to order supplies and equipment for the spring season. It is impossible to say how much money is needed to field a team, but it is possible to say that you need enough money to purchase thirty-five to fifty-five dozen tennis balls, new nets for each court, and an average of five to ten restringing jobs per player. Some schools save money by buying a stringing machine and letting the players restring their own rackets. Enough money should be allotted for shoes, socks, shirts, supporters, and trunks. Some colleges provide their players with free rackets, but that practice is declining. Travel budgets depend on the college or state policy, but mileage, meals, and housing have to be taken care of. Eating in school cafeterias and staying in guest dorms saves money.

The Fall and Spring Training Program

Tournament tennis players usually play a very demanding summer schedule. Although some coaches disagree, the fall semester should be

[2]Jim Brown, "Recruiting College Tennis Players," *Coach and Athlete*, 32, no. 11 (June, 1970) 30.

used for concentrating on studies, working on weights, and low pressure intrateam competition. Intensive fall practice and competition is unnecessary, expensive, and an overemphasis of college athletics. It can also be counterproductive because the players may become tennis weary.

Once the Christmas break is past, the real preseason conditioning program and practice sessions should begin. Whether the coach knows tennis or not, it is essential that practice sessions be established at specific times and that the coach be present. Although a few colleges have had winning teams without an active coach, their success was in spite of the coach, not because of him. College tennis players need leadership, discipline, a program, and the knowledge that they have a coach who is their own, not someone on loan from another sport on match days.

By the time dual matches begin in February or March, a routine will have been established. Organizing practices will be discussed in another part of the book. Most coaches taper off on the running program and spend more time drilling and playing during practice sessions as the season nears. As in other sports, it is advisable to avoid heavy work the day before a match, and to give your players a break in practice after especially grueling matches or tournaments.[3]

ORGANIZING PRACTICES

If there is a key to successful tennis programs in high schools and colleges other than having quality players, that key is the organization of the program. That part of the program which requires the organizational skills of the coach most is the planning and directing of productive practice sessions. Effectively organized practices are important at the high school level because the coach usually has a large number of players and a limited amount of space and time to work with them. If the coach cannot carefully plan how to use that space and time, the players are deprived of the opportunity to develop their games and the coach reduces the chances of winning tennis matches. The college coach has fewer athletes with which to deal and usually has better facilities in which to work, so he can be more flexible in organizing practices. However, the practice sessions are no less important than in high school. The college coach may be under more pressure to win, and purposeful practices can help a team achieve the goal of winning. College players may

[3]Jim Brown, "How to Go From Doorstop to Dominance in College Tennis," *Tennis Trade*, 2, no. 7 (July, 1973) 34.

have developed their fundamental skills to a high degree. Planned practices help to maintain and reinforce their playing skills and also give the players a sense of discipline and team unity not always found in the individual sports.

There are many activities from which to choose when planning practices. Some of these activities include warmup exercises, drills, singles competition, doubles competition, playing for position, free play, strategy sessions, weight training, and running. Which activities you choose to make up an individual practice period depend on the number of players on the team, the abilities of your players, their physical condition, the amount of time and space available, the time of year, and the purposes of a practice. Before considering all the activities mentioned above, here are some general suggestions for practicing team tennis.

If possible, conduct practices as a team with all members arriving and leaving at predetermined times. This is easier to do in high school because most students finish classes at about the same time. At the college level it may be harder to accomplish because students have classes at various times during the afternoon. However, if everyone knows that practice will begin at a certain time and that everyone is expected to be there, the feeling of discipline and team togetherness begins to develop. Some coaches impose penalties on team members who do not arrive at practice on time.

Make the practices enjoyable. As mentioned earlier in the book, tennis has the advantage over most sports of being a game that is fun to practice as well as to play. It is part of your responsibility to see that tennis does not lose that advantage. This philosophy does not rule out hard work such as drills and conditioning exercises. Your players will understand that their hard work is productive and will contribute toward improving their tennis playing ability. Enjoyment will come from the progress made as well as from the joy of playing. Practices can be made more enjoyable by using a variety of drills, by maintaining a balance of time spent working on fundamentals and time spent playing sets or matches, and by allowing players to practice with a variety of team members. Do not overwork your players. Plan practices that last long enough to achieve your goals for the day, but not so long that your players are too tired to eat or to study. Sessions should probably last from an hour and a half to two hours. Tournament circuit players have to put in more time than this, but tennis is their top priority. Your players should be concerned about their academic work as much as their tennis game. Give them an occasional day off. Tennis players can get stale, and a break away from the courts may help their game more than practicing.

Maintain a role as coach, observer, and director of the entire program rather than a role as a player. There are times when you can play with or against your team members such as when emulating a certain style of play or filling in as a doubles fourth. But do not compete with your players on a regular basis or try to impress them with your playing ability. If you are a good player, your students will already know it and it will do nothing for their confidence for you to beat them. If you are not a good player, you may lose their respect and you will do little to improve their skills by playing against them. Also, if you spend too much time playing during the practice sessions, you will not give enough time to the players who need your help as a teacher and coach. You cannot concentrate on your game and your players' games at the same time.

Treat all the players on the team equally. School tennis is a team matter and every player has something to contribute to the team. There is a temptation to give more time and attention to the number one and two players than to those lower in the lineup who probably need help the most. Try to promote a feeling of respect and loyalty among the players. The number one man should be just as willing to go get water for the number six man as the sixth man is for those who are better than he. Now look at some of the things that can happen in practice.

Warmup Activities

As the players begin to arrive at the courts, there are several ways for them to loosen up before beginning strenuous work. Some coaches have the players jog a quarter- or half-mile. Other coaches prefer stretching exercises and simple calisthenics for a few minutes. The most traditional and probably least effective way to warm up is by hitting. It is the easiest way to get started, but there is a tendency not to exercise all of the muscles until actual play or difficult drills begin. When that happens, there is a greater chance of muscle strains. A warmup period should be designed to prepare the athlete for strenuous activity without tiring him in the process.

Drills

Drills are an effective way to master the various mechanical components of any sport, and some time should be given to drills in almost every practice. (See Chapter 6 for tennis drills.) The problem many coaches have is in determining how much time should be given to drills and how much time should be programmed for competitive play. Some people feel that teams should spend more time drilling during the fall season or early during the spring semester before matches begin. When the schedule starts, they prefer to prepare their players for matches by spending more time in intrasquad competition. Other coaches do not share that opinion. They feel that preseason practice should consist of competition and that drills should be used during the season to prepare for specific situations or to correct problems which have developed during competition. If you are undecided about how much time to allot to drills, experiment with both methods. What works for one team or coach may not work for another. A compromise balance between drilling and playing will probably develop in each team's case.

Regardless of when drills are used and how much time is spent on drills, there are principles which apply to this segment of the practice routine. First, drills should have a purpose, and that purpose should be explained to the players. Drills should simulate game situations as much as possible. Any potential game situation or probable sequence of shots can be made into a drill. Within reason, drills should be fun. If the players dread going through some drills, it may be because the coach is not utilizing a variety of activities. Players will respond better to a variety of drills, and the response may also be better if a drill is completed while interest in it is at a peak. Players will look forward to practicing that drill the next day rather than hoping the coach will not include it in the practice schedule. Use tennis drills that are simple to explain and simple to understand. Too many x's and o's are confusing. Finally, remember to plan drills so that a progression of learning or practicing is possible. Difficult drills for beginning or intermediate players may do more to discourage them than to improve their skills.

Singles Competition

It is important that the coach plan who will play against each other in singles and doubles during practices. If the players are always allowed to make these decisions, there is the possibility that the same players will always want to play each other, that grudge matches will take up too much practice time, or that cliques will develop among the squad members. If the coach arranges the matches, he can ensure that everyone gets to practice against a variety of styles and that there is a balance of competition within the team. He can also do a better job of planning other practice segments if he knows in advance who will be available.

Doubles Competition

Practicing doubles is one of the most neglected phases of team tennis. The young players are usually more interested in the activity and challenge provided in head-to-head singles play, and the coach knows that most of the team's dual matches will involve more singles play than doubles. Consequently, practicing doubles frequently becomes something the team does after all other work is completed. The emphasis on singles is understandable, but regrettable. Doubles can be as enjoyable as singles, as rewarding, as demanding, and as important to team success. All close dual matches will be decided by what happens in doubles competition. Teams of equal strength usually split the singles matches, and the team with the best doubles combinations is in a position to win.

The point of all this information is to encourage you to spend time during practices on doubles. Try to arrange your combinations early in the preseason workouts so that teammates have time to get used to each other and to develop a successful partnership. In planning practices, allocate time for doubles work just as you do for singles, drills, and other parts of the daily routine.

Playing for Position

While doubles competition is neglected in practices, playing for positions in the lineup is overemphasized. What happens may be seen in the team that begins serious workouts for the spring season immediately after the Christmas holidays. The first few weeks are spent in conditioning and trying to regain some of the preholiday form. After that period, everyone really begins to get into a groove by working hard on strokes. All of a sudden, the first match or tournament of the season is about two or three weeks away, and the coach realizes that the lineup is not set. A round robin is hastily arranged, and everybody plays everybody else every day for two weeks. There are several problems that this approach creates. First, you probably do not have time to finish the round robin. With poor weather, weekends, missed practices, and injuries, there are just not enough days to play every match. With only eight members on a team you must play twenty-eight matches for a complete round robin tournament. The second problem is that you spend all of your practice time in competition, which forces you to neglect the other important phases of practice. There is also the possibility that an upset during the intra-squad competition could result in a lineup that does not reflect your players' true abilities. The last and most serious complication is that your players may be so tired from playing for position in practice that they cannot perform well when the season begins.

What can you do to avoid these problems? Do not commit yourself to complete a round robin tournament as the criteria for the team's lineup. Assume the responsibility of deciding yourself who will play each position. A pecking order is usually established on tennis teams, and players know how good they are and who they can beat. Therefore, the coach can arrange only the matches among players of similar ability or when there is some uncertainty about a given position. It does very little good for the number one player to play the number eight player for position, so why waste practice time letting them play. If you must play a round robin, allow plenty of time for completion before the first match. If you do not finish in time, you can do it after the season starts. Never place yourself in a position of having one match to be the only factor in determining a player's position for the season. Positions on a team should be determined by performance over a long period of time, not on what happened one day out of six months. Once the lineup has been established, it should remain stable for the season. There may be some changes as players improve or consistently defeat someone higher in the lineup, but the business of players constantly challenging each other after the schedule has begun can be time consuming, tiring, and unsettling to the team morale.

Free Play

There may be times when players on a tennis team should be free just to play for fun, but these times are limited. The whole idea of playing tennis is to play for fun, but structured play during practice can be fun. If that is not enough, there is plenty of time on weekends, at night, during holiday breaks, and during the summer for free play. If this advice sounds rather dogmatic, remember that you are coaching a varsity athletic team, not an intramural, recreation, or church league team. It is doubtful that coaches in other sports allow their players much free time during practices.

Strategy Sessions

Most tennis coaches integrate any comments they have on strategy into on-the-court work rather than making those comments in a classroom type lecture. There may be times when it is appropriate for the coach to call all of his players together to discuss a match or some phase of the game. The best time to have a group strategy meeting is immediately before a practice. Players can then put into practice the ideas just discussed.

Weight Training

Tennis players are not known as very conscientious workers when it comes to lifting weights or performing isometric exercises. They just want to play the game. Coaches frequently do not know enough about weight training to incorporate it into their programs. There are definite, tangible results possible from an organized strength building program, and most tennis players could benefit from a regimen designed for their individual needs. Weight training programs are more effective in the fall semester or early during the spring semester because there is more time for the players to work with the weights then than during the regular season. If weight work is done during the season, the goal should be to maintain levels of strength previously achieved. This can be done with a few minutes of work two or three times a week.

The type of program will vary with the individual and should be directed toward development of general muscular fitness. Tennis players will be particularly interested in increasing strength in the wrists, fore-arms, shoulders, and legs. Exercises which may be helpful in these areas are curls, push-ups, pull-ups, rope jumping, and leg presses. Some weight training can be done at the tennis courts without special equipment. Isometrics can be effective by having players swing through the various strokes to the point of probable contact. At that point of contact, one player acts as an immovable object for his partner. If an uneven number of players do the exercises, net posts or fences can serve as the objects of resistance. A daily routine of three ten second contractions at each point of contact for each stroke would be a reasonably demanding method of increasing strength. Swinging weighted rackets, two rackets simulta-neously, or rackets with covers are other effective exercises.

If you are not well enough informed about weight training to install a program, consult a physical education teacher or athletic trainer. With knowledge about the goals you want to achieve in terms of in-creasing muscular fitness and with information about your particular athletes, he should be able to advise you on how to start a program.

Running

As with the weight program, a running program should be directed toward specific goals. Most of the hard work can be done early in the year or semester, but it is common for high school and college coaches to conclude practice sessions with sprints or laps. Sprints seem to be more useful to the tennis player because the game requires starting, stopping, quick bursts of speed, running a few steps at a time, and changing directions. Running laps and cross country running may help build strength in the legs and certainly help to build pulmonary fitness, but leg strength can be increased in ways already mentioned and lung capacity is not that important in tennis. If you want to put running into your conditioning program, try sprints of ten to forty yards; wave drills in which players move forward, backward, or laterally at your command; or up-and-back drills in which players run forward at the sound of the first command, backward on the second sound, forward on the third, etc. You can design your own continuity conditioning drills by combining weight training, calisthenics, and running into five, ten, or fifteen minute continuous movement periods.

Other Considerations

Remember to take these factors into consideration before organizing practices:

1. The number of players on your team. The larger the number, the more detailed your planning must be. Have something for everybody to do at all times.

2. The abilities of your players. At the high school level, spend more time teaching fundamentals and less time playing matches. Use drills that are consistent with the talent of your players.

3. The physical condition of your players. Get them into shape before the bulk of court work begins so you can concentrate on strokes and game situations when the time comes. Give them a rest after difficult matches and do very light work the day before a match or tournament.

4. The amount of time and space available. These factors are related to the number of players on the team, but use space efficiently. There will usually be recreational tennis players waiting to use any courts not in use by the team. Allow others to use the courts as long as they do not interfere with what you are doing.

5. The time of year in relation to your schedule of matches. Organize your practice program so that your team is fresh and at its peak when interscholastic or intercollegiate competition begins or when the conference tournament is played. Do not burn them out early.

6. The specific purposes for a practice session. Have goals in mind you want to reach in every practice. Your players should leave the courts feeling that they have accomplished something.

Now that you have some ideas about what can go into a tennis practice, you must consider the alternatives and design your own program. A typical workout consists of a warm-up period followed by drills, a period of singles or doubles play, and conditioning exercises. A sample practice schedule is given below.

(Players are numbered 1 through 8; courts are lettered A through D.)

3:30	Stretching exercises	All players	Court A
3:35	Groundstroke drills	#1 and #3 #2 and #4 #5 and #7 #6 and #8	Court A Court B Court C Court D
3:50	Drills for the serve and service return	#1, #2, #3, #4 #5, #6, #7, #8	Court A Court B
4:05	Drills for the net game Singles play	#1 and #2 #3 and #4 #5 vs. #7 #6 vs. #8	Court A Court B Court C Court D
4:20	Doubles play	#1 and #2 vs. #3 and #4	Court A
5:00	Ten minutes of conditioning drills	All players	Courts A and B

Figure 4-1.

SCOUTING

Few high school or college tennis coaches have the time or the inclination to scout future opponents. Yet, the more you know about your team's opponents, the better you can prepare your players to compete with them. Since tennis teams usually see each other more than once a season either in home matches or in tournaments, it is possible to develop informative postmatch scouting reports.

For the best results, the coach should not make out formal reports himself. It is more helpful to have each player evaluate the opponent he played. Here are some advantages of postmatch, player-prepared scouting reports:

1. They may be utilized by the player in later matches if the same opponent is played.
2. They may be used the next year against returning opponents.
3. The scouting report forces the players on your team to be conscious of the opponents' style of play.

4. The reports encourage some players to evaluate their own styles more closely.

5. They consume less time than a report prepared by the coach on each opponent.

6. The reports may stimulate a higher degree of interest among some of your players.

The scouting report form should be short, simple, and easy to read. Although each coach can prepare a form that is best for his situation, certain basic information must be included. That information consists of the opponent's name and school, the date of the match, the type of surface played on, and the weather conditions. The first section is followed by information concerning each of the opponent's strokes, his strongest shots, weakest shots, unusual shots, quickness, strength, and endurance. The report concludes with comments on the opponent's honesty in making calls and his style of play, and an overall evaluation of his game.

Elaborate scouting reports should be avoided. Most players would rather play the game than analyze it. They should prepare the reports as soon after a match as possible, while the shots and situations are still fresh in their minds. After a match away from home, the reports can be completed during the trip back. For home matches, the players can take the forms home and return them at practice the next day.

How can the information be used best? First, the files should be stored in the coach's office and made accessible to every player. The team members should be encouraged to come in on their own to read about future opponents. Two players who have faced a mutual opponent might compare notes, or the coach might review a report with an individual player, possibly making additions and modifications. The reports can also be discussed at team meetings. This will help promote team unity and give less experienced or observant players an opportunity to listen to the observations made by their teammates.

Coaches should not expect a wealth of new information from the reports. If each player can observe and record a single strength, weakness, or characteristic of an opponent (or himself), the report will be worth the effort. The benefits from postmatch scouting are more subjective than objective, and are more difficult to measure. The reward may come months or even years later.

The form shown in this chapter was designed for relatively experienced players. For younger, less analytic players, a multiple choice type of questionnaire can be developed. For example, "What was your opponent's style of play, (1) Serve and volley, (2) retriever-pusher, (3) unorthodox, (4) no special style?"

Tennis Scouting Report

Player __STEVE HORNSBY__ School __BROADMOOR H.S.__

Date of Match __4-15-75__ Reported by __JOE PENDAS__

Results __PENDAS__ (def.) lost to __HORNSBY__

Score __6-4, 3-6, 7-6__ Type of Court __CONCRETE__

Weather __HOT, HUMID, NO WIND__ (RH)/ LH ____

Attitude __SERIOUS; NO CHATTER__

Forehand __CONSISTENT, BUT NOT POWERFUL__

Backhand __BACKSPIN; CAN GO DOWN THE LINE OR C.C.__

First Serve __GOES TO OUTSIDE MOST OF THE TIME__

Second Serve __TWIST, SLOW, SHALLOW__

Net Game __GOOD VOLLEYER; NO DROP SHOTS;__
__ERRATIC OVERHEAD; BLOWS SOME SET-UPS__

Best Shot __FOREHAND VOLLEY__

Weakest Shot __SECOND SERVE__

Unusual Shots __—__

Quickness __HARD TO PASS AT NET__ Strength __AVERAGE__

Endurance __TIRES IN THIRD__ Speed __BETTER THAN AVG.__

Calls __HONEST; GAVE ME CLOSE ONES__

Style of Play __STEADY; SMOOTH; CAN SERVE + VOLLEY__

Overall Evaluation __STRONG NO.3 MAN; WILL IMPROVE;__
__MATCH COULD HAVE GONE EITHER__
__WAY.__

Figure 4-2.

Since scouting is practically nonexistent in tennis, and since players always exchange comments about opponents, it makes sense to channel these observations into written scouting reports. Even if the reports produce no significant information, they will give the players an increased awareness of the various aspects of the game.[4]

[4]Jim Brown, "Post-Match Scouting in Tennis," *Scholastic Coach*, 43, no. 7 (March, 1974) 74.

PUBLICIZING SCHOOL TEAMS

High school and college teams, even good ones, may go virtually unnoticed by a community and by the student body unless those teams are promoted by the coach, players, and the people responsible for sports publicity. But a well publicized tennis program draws spectators to matches, keeps the name of the school before the public, promotes the game, and serves as a recruiting technique for other players and students.

Publicizing a tennis team presents some problems not found in other interscholastic and intercollegiate sports. First, tennis is a sport most people would rather play than watch. Only a handful of schools throughout the country draw large crowds for dual matches. The saturation approach being used by television is also driving people out of their dens and onto tennis courts to play, not to watch. Second, tennis matches are difficult to cover, especially if the sports writer is not familiar with the sport. Play by play accounts are impossible, and most dual matches last two to three hours. Also, there may be as many as six matches being played at one time, so that detailed coverage of more than the number one singles and doubles matches is not practical. Finally, tennis has to compete with the other spring sports—baseball, track, and golf—for space on the sports pages. Many sports editors may assume that their readers are more interested in these sports than in tennis. Following are some suggestions on how to minimize these problems.

The coach has some specific responsibilities regarding the publicity his team receives. The first rule is to forget about modesty when it comes to your team's activities and achievements. If you have a team worth promoting, tell people about it—especially sports writers, sports editors, and sports information directors. Remember that they have several other sports to cover, and there is a good chance that if you do not tell them what is happening with your team, no one else will. Look for angles they might use in publicizing your players and schedule. Do not be above writing your own press releases and turning them in to the sports publicity person, a newspaper, or a news bureau for polishing and distribution. If you write a story, put the who, what, where, and when information in the lead sentence of the first paragraph. The remaining parts of the story come in subsequent paragraphs, which should not exceed three or four sentences in newspapers. The more important the information, the closer it should be to the top of the article.

The second rule is to keep accurate records during dual matches and tournaments, and to be prompt in reporting results to the sports information officer or to local newspapers, radio and television stations. Newspapers will usually take full accounts of the competition, while television reporters want just the final results plus a few highlights. Prompt reporting is especially important for out of town matches. If you do not call the results in before leaving on your return trip, make sure that arrangements to do so have been made with someone associated with the host school.

Even the players can share in publicizing home matches. Many schools have their players put up leaflets around the campus the day before a home match. The posters or leaflets should be simple, easy to read, and should contain only vital information. Here is an example:

```
TENNIS
MCNEESE VS. LAMAR
TUESDAY – 1:30
```

The players may balk at this idea at first, but they know they would prefer to play before a crowd, and the leaflets probably inform more people who have the time to attend a match on short notice than any other medium. Home matches may also be publicized on public billboards, bulletin boards, and marquees (See Figure 4-3).

The primary responsibility of tennis publicity at the college level belongs to the sports information director or to a person assigned by the campus news bureau. The person in this position can do as much to make or break a program as anyone. He should give the tennis team the time and effort consistent with the quality of the program and consistent with the time, effort, and space given to other spring sports.

The first tennis story of the year is usually one announcing the team's schedule. The number of matches and tournaments to be played, the opening date, extended road trips, teams expected to provide the best competition, and the district or conference outlook are possible leads. The second story is often a season preview in which information is given about returning team members, freshmen and transfers are introduced to the readers, and the coach's outlook for the season is described.

Prior to the beginning of the season, which is usually in February or March, schedule cards or spring sports brochures should be prepared and distributed. Local businesses may be interested in financing the printing in return for an advertisement on the handout. The cards and brochures can be placed at points around the campus or at businesses interested in the school. Brochures should be mailed to area news media

Figure 4-3. Using a public marquee to publicize a home match.

and to the coach or athletic department of all opponents. In addition to printed material, someone should arrange to have head shots and action photographs made of each player. The pictures can be used with stories throughout the season.

Once the season begins, two to four articles a week should be distributed through the high school newspaper or the college news bureau. Most news bureaus can get stories to every newspaper and most radio and television stations in a state or area of the state. A tennis mailing list should not only be maintained for the media, but also for anyone interested in your program. College coaches can send news releases to high school prospects. Most teams average two matches a week, and if practical, articles should go out in advance and be followed by news stories giving match results. Morning papers prefer a straight news account of a match, while afternoon papers will be looking for an angle, since the match results might be old news by the time the paper is circulated.

Developing an angle for a routine match can be difficult. Team or individual winning streaks, conference matches, or outstanding efforts by some team member might provide material for a lead. Feature articles on players are easier to develop. It is a good idea to have at least one article and photograph per player each season, and the release should be sent to the player's hometown newspaper. Possible leads for player oriented features include the tennis background of team members, summer tennis results (many players play on some kind of summer circuit), the academic achievements of players (tennis players tend to make higher grades than other athletes), and at the college level, the foreign player angle. There are hundreds of foreign players in American colleges and universities, and possibilities for stories are almost unlimited. Why did they come to this particular school, how were they recruited, what about the language problems, what adjustments had to be made, how do tennis and academic programs in the two countries compare, and what happens after graduation are examples of questions that can lead to interesting stories. Foreign players give an added dimension to college athletics, and frequently develop a following of their own at matches and in the community.

Most newspapers run a weekly sports column, and the writer is usually looking for filler type material. It might as well be about tennis, and the information can come from the coach or the SID. The sports publicity director and the coach should also maintain yearly tennis records. The records include team and individual performances, and can be used in brochures and summary type news releases (for example, each player's dual match won-lost record, a coach's overall won-lost record, or long term district or conference performances). Occasionally, local newspapers can write follow-up stories on former players. Many high school players go on to play college tennis and some college players become teaching professionals and coaches.

There are other details about a program that each tennis coach must apply to his or her situation. Not every high school has a newspaper and not every college has a sports information director, so the coach may have a dual role to perform. Whatever the situation, do not assume that if your team wins, the publicity will take care of itself. In tennis, it just does not work that way. People will know about a good program only when the coach, the players, the sports writers, and the school are interested enough to promote the team using every available technique.[5]

[5]Louis Bonnette and Jim Brown, "Publicizing a Collegiate Tennis Program," *Tennis Trade*, 3, no. 3 (March, 1974) 20.

TREATING TENNIS INJURIES

High school and college tennis coaches frequently have to serve as first aid dispensers and athletic trainers. Fortunately, most tennis injuries do not involve emergencies, so coaches who have some information about taking care of common tennis injuries can give reasonably adequate treatment and advice about further medical care. Because most athletic injuries occur during practice sessions, it is a good idea to have a well equipped first aid kit at the courts every day. Most coaches are conscientious about seeing that the kit is there for matches, but few coaches take the trouble to prepare for injuries during practices.

While tennis elbow gets most of the publicity, there are several less serious but more common problems among tennis players. Blisters, sprains, strains, cramps, and shin splints are examples of tennis injuries almost all players have encountered.

Blisters

Beginning players and those who have not played for a while are probably going to have blisters on the racket hand and on the feet, in that order. A blister is an accumulation of fluid between the top two layers of skin. Blisters are caused by irritation; in this case, irritation between the racket and the hand, and between the foot and the sock, shoe, or court.

Some blisters can be avoided by following this advice: (1) Require your players to play for only short periods of time when beginning a practice season and gradually increase the amount of playing time as they become physically tougher. The people who practice or play for two or three hours the first day out are certain to get blisters. (2) Make sure that the racket grip is the right size for the player's hand. Rackets with grips that are too large or too small will increase the amount of friction. (3) Keep the racket handle as dry as possible. The more slippage, the greater the chance of irritation to the hand. (4) Wear a tennis glove or tape on the areas of the hand most likely to blister. Although many players feel that they lose their touch if they have something between the hand and the racket, a glove may be worn until the hand becomes tough, then the glove will not be needed. (5) To avoid blisters on the feet, put talcum powder on the feet, wear shoes that fit, and wear two pairs of socks.

Once blisters develop, follow this procedure: Clean the area with alcohol or soap and water, sterilize a needle, and make an opening at the base of the blister so that the fluid can drain. Then place a bandage over the entire area. Some players can play with the pain caused by blisters and others cannot. If your players continue to play, keep the first aid supplies nearby, because the areas on the hands and feet likely to blister are difficult to bandage, and the bandage will come off as the players move and perspire. In some cases, the top layer of skin should be removed, but this should only be done by a trainer or physician.

Sprains

A sprain is an injury to a joint which usually damages blood vessels, ligaments, and tendons in the area. A sprain is frequently caused by forcing a joint beyond the normal range of motion. In tennis, the most common sprains occur in the ankles. If the ankle is sprained, the symptoms will be swelling, tenderness, pain upon motion or when weight is placed on the injured joint, and discoloration. It is possible for a fracture to occur at the same time as a sprain. The degree of pain should not be a factor in trying initially to determine whether or not a break has occurred. Sprains may be more painful than fractures.

If a player sprains an ankle, do three things: Put pressure on the ankle with a wrap; put ice or some other cold application on the affected joint; and elevate the leg. All three first aid measures will reduce the amount of fluid rushing to the area, thus reducing swelling and pain. Continue the cold applications up to twenty-four hours or until the swelling and bleeding subside. An elastic wrap will provide pressure without cutting off circulation. After the first twenty-four hours, apply warm compresses to the area to stimulate circulation and healing. Do not allow your players to start playing too soon after a sprain. Joints sprained once seem to be more susceptible to subsequent sprains. When the injured player does resume play, the ankle may be taped for support.

Strains

Strains are tears in muscle tissue and connective tissue. Strains are also called pulled muscles and muscle tears. They may be caused by overexertion, sudden movement, fatigue, and improper warmup. In tennis, the most likely parts of the body to be affected by strains are the legs, back, and the wrist. The symptoms will probably be sharp pain when the injured muscles are exercised, general soreness, and muscle spasms. Rest, heat, and massage are used to treat strains, although the massage technique could be painful. Trainers, therapists, and physicians may treat pulled muscles by ultrasound and whirlpool bath methods. If the back muscles are involved, the player should sleep on a firm surface so that the sore muscles are not stretched further. If the wrist is strained, taping can give support and reduce the pain. The player who suffers a strain can usually return to practice sooner than one who has a sprain.

Heat Cramps

Heat cramps usually affect tennis players in the legs, arms, or hands. The cramps are involuntary contractions of muscles, and they could be caused by fatigue, high temperature, loss of body salt, and overexertion of muscles. Pressure and warm wraps may alleviate the immediate discomfort, but many cramps could be avoided by progressive conditioning programs, adequate salt and water intake before and during periods of exercise, and rest periods during practice sessions.

Shin Splints

A shin splint causes pain and discomfort in the lower leg. The injury may be an inflammation of the tissue between the two bones of the lower leg, an inflammation of muscles in the lower leg, or a muscle spasm. Shin splints could be caused by running on hard surfaces, by playing on different surfaces, by poor conditioning, poor running techniques, or abnormalities in the skeletal structure.

Tennis players are more likely to suffer from shin splints early in the season, especially if practices are held on a hard surface. The treatment for this kind of injury is taping to elevate and support the arch, using a foam rubber cushion in the heel of the shoe, taking aspirin before and after running, and soaking the leg in ice water for about fifteen minutes after running. If the pain is severe, the only other treatment is rest. Shin splints may be avoided by a thorough conditioning program for players and by short practice sessions at the beginning of the season so players can adjust to running on hard surfaces.

Tennis Elbow

Tennis elbow has been written about extensively during the past five years, so there is much more information on the subject than will be presented here. One of the most thorough treatments of the subject appeared in the March 1974 issue of *Tennis* magazine. Causes, prevention, and cures are discussed in a series of articles.

Tennis elbow is an inflammation of the tissue around the end of the bone in the upper arm at the elbow. It could be caused by the constant impact of the ball on the racket, causing stress in the forearm muscles, by improper technique on certain strokes, by weak muscles, or by heavy and tightly strung rackets. The primary symptom of tennis elbow is pain in the elbow area. The pain may occur only on certain shots or in certain positions of the arm, but if the injury is serious enough, there may be pain to the touch and even pain when one shakes hands or brushes one's teeth.

There are many types of treatment, but no single method is effective for everyone. If one of your players develops tennis elbow, get advice and treatment from a trainer or physician. Some of the treatment methods that have been successful include the use of cold packs to reduce inflammation, rest, medicines such as aspirin and cortisone to relieve the irritation, heat, massage, elbow braces, and even surgery. If you are coaching a school team, your players probably will not be bothered by tennis elbow problems. Middle aged players account for more than half of those who get tennis elbow.

5 *Directing Programs*

ORGANIZING AND DIRECTING COMPETITION

Before tennis competition can be held, many decisions must be made. These decisions may be made by the tennis administrator such as a coach, club pro, camp sports director, or recreation coordinator, or a tournament steering committee may be formed to consider recommendations and to make the necessary decisions.

Among the decisions which must be considered in the early planning stage is which kind of tournament to conduct. The most common forms of tennis tournaments are the single elimination, the single elimination with a consolation bracket, the round robin, the ladder, and the pyramid. The single elimination format is used when there is a large number of participants present at one site and not much time available to complete the competition. Round robins, ladders, and pyramids are used when continuous competition over a period of weeks or months is the objective. Each of these forms of competition will be discussed in detail later in this chapter.

The tournament director or committee must also make some decisions early about money. How much money will be needed for the tournament? Where will the money come from? Will the players be charged entry fees? If so, how much? Will tennis balls be supplied by tournament officials or by the players? How many and what type of awards must be purchased?

A decision must be made regarding facilities. Are there enough courts available to accommodate the number of players expected to enter the tournament? Are the courts in good enough condition to conduct formal competition? Are there additional courts available within a reasonable distance of the primary tournament site should they be needed?

The committee has to decide who is eligible to compete in this event. Will the tournament be open to people of all ages or will there be divisions for juniors, adults, junior veterans, and seniors? Is the competition to be for men, women, or both? Will participants have to be affiliated with a club, organization, or school to be eligible? Will entries be restricted to residents of a city, state, or region? Will the tournament be open to players of all levels, or will there be divisions for novices and advanced players?

In addition to the general format of competition, the specific form that individual matches will take must be determined. Will play be restricted to singles, or will there be doubles and mixed doubles? Will matches consist of pro sets, two out of three sets, three out of five sets, or some other arrangement? If tie-breakers are to be used, which method would be appropriate? Will there be a forfeit time allowed to participants? If so, how long? How many events will a player be allowed to enter?

How much time will be necessary to complete the tournament? Will the tournament schedule interfere with any other tennis activities planned for the courts? Will there be other athletic, social, business, or educational events which may conflict with the dates planned for the tournament?

Finally, are there enough people who are qualified and willing to conduct the tournament? It is not difficult to find lots of people who would enjoy hosting or participating in a tennis event. It is very difficult to find these people when the work of planning and conducting competition begins. So, once the preliminary decisions regarding the tournament have been made, volunteer workers must be recruited, coordinated, and supervised. Besides the tournament steering committee, there may be a need to organize others into committees to help coordinate various efforts. The people on these committees should be enlisted and told about their responsibilities as much as six months prior to a tournament in which there will be a large number of participants. This is especially true of the open single elimination tournament with many out of town players. Junior age division events also need special preparation and involvement of much of the tennis community. Here are possible committee titles and suggestions for those who serve on the committees.

Tournament Committee

This committee has responsibilities in addition to deciding on the type of tournament, funding, facilities, and eligibility. If the tournament is to be sanctioned by the United States Tennis Association or any other organization, the committee should make a request for sanctioning and for playing dates. These requests must be made prior to yearly deadlines already established by each sanctioning organization. If local sponsorship by a club, civic group, or school is necessary, the tournament steering committee should seek such support a year to six months before the tournament is tentatively scheduled.

Registration Committee

The registration committee is responsible for registering participants when they first arrive at a tournament, and the same group can also be asked to prepare and distribute entry blanks. Entry blanks should be distributed a month to three weeks before the date of the tournament, and players should return the forms at least one week before the event begins. An entry blank should contain rules and information about the tournament, a schedule of events, space for vital information about the entrant, a list of events in which the player may indicate his plans for participation, the address to which the entry form and fees may be mailed, and a statement releasing the tournament officials from responsibility for damages, losses, or injuries sustained during the tournament.

Registration of players usually begins the day before a tournament starts and continues until all players have reported in and doubles entries have closed. Registration tables should be placed at a central location near the courts. Specific instructions should be given to the registration workers about their duties and the times they are expected to be at the tables. Players will have been notified to report to the registration area when they arrive. The registrars should have some system of recording the names of players who have checked in. Entry fees may also be collected and doubles entries accepted at the registration site. Finally, workers may be asked to give the registering players information about housing, and to tell them where the brackets have been posted.

Competition Committee

A competition committee may be established for the purpose of seeing that matches are played on schedule and according to the rules. A tournament referee heads the committee and is the principal authority in matters related to play for the tournament as a whole. Umpires and linespersons may also serve on this committee. Umpires oversee individual matches by introducing players to the audience, keeping score, repeating linespersons' calls, and generally seeing that a given match proceeds normally. Linespersons are assigned to watch specific boundary lines on the court and to make calls of "out" or "fault" when necessary. These officials may also be responsible for calling foot faults on the server.

Tennis Balls Committee

This committee may seem to have rather limited responsibilities, but some tournament directors assign one or two persons with the tasks of pricing and purchasing tennis balls for the event. Enough balls should be purchased to provide new ones for each match played, and if possible, new balls should be given to players who play a third set. It is better to overorder balls than to risk not having enough to complete a tournament. Some dealers may allow for the unused balls to be returned and the money refunded. This committee may collect used balls after matches have been completed, and then sell the balls or distribute them in some other manner.

Transportation Committee

For junior tournaments and some open events, a transportation committee may be needed. This group of people can be responsible for transporting players among various court sites or for getting players from the courts to private homes, motels, or dormitories. Station wagons and vans can be used by this committee more effectively than city buses because there are seldom more than three or four players to be moved from one place to another at a time. Departure times from sites should be posted at the courts. The transportation committee must work closely with the housing committee.

Housing Committee

Many tournaments for junior players still provide housing in private homes for participants. The person who serves as the committee director must be one who can persuade others to house players, one who is very efficient in handling details, and one who is willing to do as much or more work than anyone involved with the tournament. An experienced housing committee chairperson has given these suggestions for others who accept the same responsibility: (1) Begin compiling a list of persons willing to serve as hosts at least two months before the tournament begins. (2) When requests for housing are received, send a letter to the person making the request stating the provisions of being housed and giving the names and addresses of the hosts. Try to arrange all housing at least one week before the starting date. (3) Do not allow arrangements to be made by calling the housing director or committee members. (4) See that arrangements are made for the hosts and visitors to meet when the players arrive for registration. (5) Maintain a card file containing the names and vital information for all players who will be housed. (6) Save all material for future reference.

Publicity Committee

The people on the publicity committee are responsible for all public information about the tournament before, during, and after the event. They should get to know members of the press personally and provide them with stories or ideas about every phase of the tournament. During the tournament a copy of the bracket with winners' names circled should be provided to reporters. Publicity committee members may also call in results to newspapers in cities represented by players in the tournament. All news releases and other printed matter related to the tournament should be kept for future use.

Entertainment Committee

Some tournaments provide junior players with free tickets to theaters, bowling lanes, and miniature golf courses. Cookouts, beach parties, and dances are also popular forms of entertainment for younger players. However, keep in mind that players will be on or around the courts all day, and that competition may not be completed until well into the evening. Many well-intentioned plans for entertainment have not materialized because the participants of the tournament were not able to attend or were too tired. The trend is toward fewer extratournament entertainment activities.

Awards Committee

Awards such as trophies, plaques, and ribbons are usually presented to first and second place finishers in each division. A sportsmanship award is also frequently awarded. The people responsible for ordering trophies or other items should allow for a two-or three-week delivery time. The committee chairperson or tournament director should have the awards before the tournament begins. Local businesses may be willing to sponsor awards.

After all of these arrangements have been made, there must be at least one person who knows the mechanics of structuring the various kinds of tournaments previously mentioned. That person may be the tournament director, the umpire, or someone else. If you are a coach, teacher, or program director, you will probably be the one expected to do the work of drawing up the tournament pairings. Here are descriptions and procedures for organizing and directing five kinds of tournaments.

Single Elimination

The basic idea of the single elimination tournament is that players' names are drawn and placed on lines in a tournament bracket. Matches are played between players whose names appear on connected bracket lines. Winners of those matches advance to another round of competition, and losers are eliminated from the tournament. There are many contingencies which will be discussed in the step-by-step description of how to draw up this type of tournament. Single elimination tournaments are probably the most common method used to determine tennis championships. The advantages of this format are its familiarity among players, its simplicity, and the short amount of time needed to complete play. The primary disadvantage is that approximately half the participants get to play only one match in each division they enter. Following are instructions for setting up a single elimination bracket.

Step #1. Determine the number of participants. Entry blanks or sign up sheets will have been distributed and returned by a stipulated date. The tournament may be open to as many people who care to enter or the field may be limited to a certain number of players.

Step #2. Determine the number of lines needed to arrange first round matches, draw up the bracket sheet, and number the lines in the first vertical column. The number of lines will be 2, 4, 8, 16, 32, 64, or 128, depending on the number of participants. The next highest power of two above the number of participants will be the number of first round bracket lines needed. For example, if twelve people enter the tournament, a sixteen line bracket will be used. If there are twenty-eight entries, a thirty-two line bracket is necessary. Brackets may be constructed manually, or printed brackets may be available from sporting goods companies.

Step #3. Determine the number of first round byes and place them in the bracket. If the number of entries does not equal an exact power of two, some players will not have to play a first round match. By receiving a bye (not having to play in that round), a player advances to the next round. This system ensures that the number of players in the next round will equal an exact power of two, thus eliminating the need for byes after round one.

To determine the number of byes, subtract the number of entries from the number of lines in the bracket. For example, if there are twenty-five players entered in a tournament, the bracket will have thirty-two lines. There would be seven first round byes. If the event is sanctioned by the United States Tennis Association, there are specific guidelines to follow in placing the byes. These guidelines are given in that organization's literature. Other organizations such as school athletic conferences may have their own set of rules for placing byes in the bracket. Figures 5-1 and 5-2 illustrate two methods of placing byes in a thirty-two line bracket. In the first bracket (Figure 5-1), there are twenty-eight entries and four byes. The byes are separated by placement in each of the four quarters of the bracket.

In the second bracket (Figure 5-2), there are twenty-seven entries and five byes. The byes are placed on every other line beginning with the second line up from the bottom and the second line down from the top. The larger uneven number of byes (three, in this case) is placed in the bottom half of the bracket.

Step #4. Determine the number of rounds to be played. A round is a stage in the bracket through which players must advance. In an eight line bracket, there will be three rounds; in a sixteen line bracket, four rounds; in a thirty-two line bracket, five rounds; in a sixty-four line bracket, six rounds; and in a bracket of one hundred and twenty-eight lines, seven rounds. With this information, a player can tell how many matches must be won to reach a certain level in the event.

Step #5. Determine the total number of matches to be played in the tournament. That number will be one less than the total number of participants. Knowing how many matches will be played will help you in scheduling matches.

Step #6. Determine the number of first round matches. This number can be calculated by subtracting the number of byes from the number of participants in the tournament and dividing the result by two. For example, if seven players enter the tournament, there will be one bye. One from seven equals six; six divided by two equals three first round matches. This information is also necessary before scheduling can begin.

Step #7. Determine the number and names of seeded players. Seeded players are those whose past record indicates that they will be the best players in the tournament. By seeding, or placing their names in the bracket rather than drawing the names of all players, you can avoid the possibility of the best competitors facing each other early in the tournament. If seeds receive byes, others have the opportunity to play against opponents of similar ability before meeting the best players. Seeding also makes it more likely that outstanding players will be competing in the later rounds of the tournament, which is desirable for attracting spectators. The U.S.T.A. stipulates that in events which it sponsors, no more than one out of every four players entered in the tournament may be seeded. Fewer than that number may be seeded, or no players at all may be seeded.

1. Pitko
*2. Bye
3. Foster
4. Judkins
5. Merki
6. Thomas
7. Nassar
8. Soulier
9. Ruhl
10. Covin
11. Sparks
12. Callender
13. St. George
14. Scott
*15. Bye
16. Brand
17. Guillory
*18. Bye
19. Morgan
20. Moore
21. Garbo
22. Byles
23. Steck
24. Black
25. Norris
26. Sahlman
27. Campbell
28. Harlow
29. Peterson
30. Lyons
*31. Bye
32. Bailey

Figure 5-1. Placement of four byes* in separate bracket quarters in a field of twenty-eight players.

Figure 5-2. Placement of five byes* from bottom and top of bracket respectively, in a field of twenty-seven players.

Step #8. Determine where the seeded players will be placed in the bracket and write in their names. There is more than one way this can be done. If the tournament is informal, the tournament director may use any system that is fair and that has been agreed upon by the participants. If the event is controlled by school or conference rules, they must be followed. If the tournament is sanctioned by the U.S.T.A., the instructions are very specific. In the bracket shown in Figure 5-3, a coin flip is used to determine the placement of four seeded players in a thirty-two line bracket. A coin is flipped to decide whether the number one seed goes on line one or line thirty-two. The number two seed is placed on the line not filled. Another coin is tossed to determine whether the third seeded player goes to line nine or line twenty-four. The fourth seed is placed on the line not filled by the third seed.

Step #9. Draw for the remaining positions and place the players' names on the bracket lines. As each name is drawn, it is written on the first open line starting from the top of the bracket. If names of two players from the same school or city are drawn to play each other in a first round match, the tournament director may place the second name on the first open line in the bottom half of the bracket.

Step #10. Write in days, times, and court assignments. This information should be inserted into the space between the names of the two players who are to compete against each other. Information for all first and second round matches should be posted, as well as information regarding days, times, and court assignment for matches in subsequent rounds. The scheduling of matches in later rounds may be done as the first round matches are completed or at the end of the first and second days of play.

All of the preparatory work on the bracket should be completed at least twenty-four hours before the tournament begins. Figure 5-4 shows a thirty-two line bracket filled out and ready for the tournament to begin.

Step #11. Begin play. As the players arrive at the courts, give court assignments, match balls, and instructions for reporting scores and returning used balls.

Step #12. As matches are completed, record scores, collect used balls, and tell the players when and where their next matches will be played. Names of winning players are written on the appropriate line in the next round, and scores are written below the lines.

Step #13. Determine time and court assignments for any matches not already scheduled and write the assignments on the bracket.

Step #14. Record scores and collect used balls as the remaining

Figure 5-3. Placement of the names of four seeded players in a thirty-two line bracket as determined by a coin toss.

Figure 5-4. Thirty-two line bracket for twenty-seven entries as the bracket would appear prior to the beginning of play.

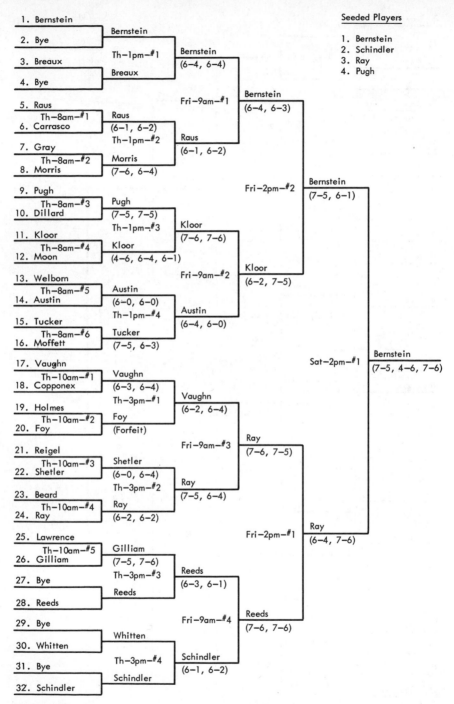

Figure 5-5. Thirty-two line bracket for twenty-seven entries as the bracket would appear after completion of play.

matches are completed. Figure 5-5 illustrates a thirty-two line bracket as it would appear after the tournament had been completed.

Single Elimination With a Consolation Bracket

The single elimination tournament with a consolation or losers' bracket ensures that each participant will play at least two matches. This format is especially useful when there are sixteen entries or less. The method of placing names and byes is the same as for the straight single elimination tournament. Players who lose in the first round of championship competition move into a separate bracket which is then played out from the start as a completely different tournament. The winners advance and the losers are eliminated. A consolation champion is determined.

There are two ways to draw up the brackets. The first method is to post a completely separate draw sheet for the consolation participants. As players lose first round matches in championship play, insert their names in the consolation bracket from top to bottom as they appeared on the original bracket. This method is shown in Figure 5-6.

Another way to establish the pairings for the losers' bracket is to construct the bracket adjacent and to the left of the championship draw. As first round matches are completed, the names of winners move into the right (championship) side of the bracket while the names of losers move to the left side. This arrangement is illustrated in Figure 5-7. Days, times, and court assignments must be inserted just as in any other type of bracket.

Round Robin

In a round robin tournament, every player or team plays every other player or team once. The winner of the competition is the player or team finishing play with the best won-lost record. This form of competition is especially suitable for interscholastic competition and city tennis leagues. As with the single elimination tournament, decisions must be made regarding the format of competition, eligibility, entry fees, provisions for balls, etc. Here is a step-by-step procedure for scheduling and conducting matches in a round robin tournament.

Step #1. Determine the number of participants.

Step #2. Determine the total number of matches to be played. This can be done by multiplying the number of participants by one less than the number of participants and dividing the result by two. For example, if there are ten entries, ten multiplied by nine equals ninety; ninety divided by two equals forty-five. There will be forty-five matches played

Championship Bracket

Consolation Bracket

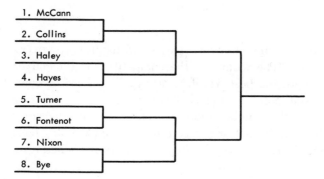

Figure 5-6. Single elimination tournament with a separate consolation bracket.

in a single round robin tournament with ten entries. If a formula will help you to remember how to establish the total number of matches, the formula is $\dfrac{N(N-1)}{2}$, with N representing the number of participants.

Consolation Bracket   Championship Bracket

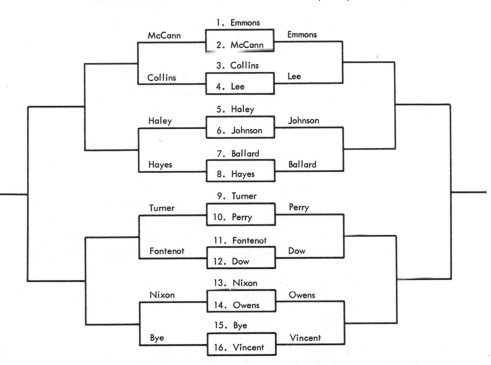

Figure 5-7. Single elimination tournament with an adjacent consolation bracket.

Step #3. Assign a number to each player or team and list the numbers and names at the top of the schedule sheet.

Step #4. Determine the arrangement of matches to be played. If there is an even number of participants, list their corresponding numbers in two vertical columns as shown in Figure 5-8. The numbers will be separated by the "vs." abbreviation. The numbers represent the names of first round opponents.

To arrange pairings for the second round, leave the number "1" stationary and rotate all other numbers one place in a counter-clockwise motion. Continue the rotation, moving the numbers one place for each subsequent round of play until the original arrangement of numbers has been reached. A completed round robin arrangement of pairings for an even number of players is shown in Figure 5–9.

If there is an odd number of players, place the word "Bye" in the upper left corner of the vertical listing of players' numbers. As the numbers are rotated for each round of play, the "Bye" remains stationary. Players or teams whose numbers appear opposite the "Bye" have an

Team Names

1.	Aces	5.	Pushers
2.	Racketeers	6.	Netters
3.	Foot Faulters	7.	Slammers
4.	Rockets	8.	Letters

1 vs. 8
2 vs. 7
3 vs. 6
4 vs. 5

Figure 5-8. First round pairings in a round robin tournament with an even number of participants.

open date. A completed round robin arrangement of pairings for an odd number of entries is illustrated in Figure 5-10.

Step #5. Determine and write in days, times, and court assignments for each match. If these factors create an advantage for a player or team, rearrange the order of matches in each round in a way that will negate the possible advantage. A sample round robin schedule is shown in Figure 5-11.

Team Names

1.	Aces	5.	Pushers
2.	Racketeers	6.	Netters
3.	Foot Faulters	7.	Slammers
4.	Rockets	8.	Letters

First Round
1 vs. 8
2 vs. 7
3 vs. 6
4 vs. 5

Second Round
1 vs. 7
8 vs. 6
2 vs. 5
3 vs. 4

Third Round
1 vs. 6
7 vs. 5
8 vs. 4
2 vs. 3

Fourth Round
1 vs. 5
6 vs. 4
7 vs. 3
8 vs. 2

Fifth Round
1 vs. 4
5 vs. 3
6 vs. 2
7 vs. 8

Sixth Round
1 vs. 3
4 vs. 2
5 vs. 8
6 vs. 7

Seventh Round
1 vs. 2
3 vs. 8
4 vs. 7
5 vs. 6

Figure 5-9. Completed round robin arrangement of pairings for an even number of participants.

Team Names
1. Lake Charles   5. Moss Bluff
2. Sulphur   6. Iowa
3. West Lake   7. Vinton
4. Maplewood

First Round			Fifth Round		
Bye	vs.	7	Bye	vs.	3
1	vs.	6	4	vs.	2
2	vs.	5	5	vs.	1
3	vs.	4	6	vs.	7

Second Round			Sixth Round		
Bye	vs.	6	Bye	vs.	2
7	vs.	5	3	vs.	1
1	vs.	4	4	vs.	7
2	vs.	3	5	vs.	6

Third Round			Seventh Round		
Bye	vs.	5	Bye	vs.	1
6	vs.	4	2	vs.	7
7	vs.	3	3	vs.	6
1	vs.	2	4	vs.	5

Fourth Round		
Bye	vs.	4
5	vs.	3
6	vs.	2
7	vs.	1

Figure 5-10. Completed round robin arrangement of pairings for an odd number of participants.

Step #6. Begin play. The only thing left to do is the day to day supervision of competition. Someone must be designated to see that play runs smoothly, to record results, to maintain league standings, and to see the tournament through to the end.

Ladder

A ladder tournament is one in which the names of players are listed vertically and numbered consecutively from the top to the bottom of the list. The positions of the players may be initially determined by chance or may be listed according to ability. A participant may challenge another player who is ranked one or two positions above the challenger. If the challenger wins the match, he changes places with the defeated player. Players should not be allowed to challenge the same person twice within a short period of time, and no player should be required to play more than one match per week or other stipulated period of time. Results of challenge matches must be reported within a specified period of time, and the tournament director must post all changes in

Player's Names
1. Savoy

Player's Names

1. Savoy	5. Bond
2. Powell	6. Adams
3. Gary	7. Cotten
4. LeBato	8. Porter

First Round

1	vs.	8	Mon – June 1st – 6:00 – Court #1
2	vs.	7	Mon – June 1st – 6:00 – Court #2
3	vs.	6	Mon – June 1st – 8:00 – Court #1
4	vs.	5	Mon – June 1st – 8:00 – Court #2

Second Round

1	vs.	7	Wed – June 3rd – 6:00 – Court #1
8	vs.	6	Wed – June 3rd – 6:00 – Court #2
2	vs.	5	Wed – June 3rd – 8:00 – Court #1
3	vs.	4	Wed – June 3rd – 8:00 – Court #2

Third Round

1	vs.	6	Fri – June 5th – 6:00 – Court #1
7	vs.	5	Fri – June 5th – 6:00 – Court #2
8	vs.	4	Fri – June 5th – 8:00 – Court #1
2	vs.	3	Fri – June 5th – 8:00 – Court #2

* Fourth Round

7	vs.	3	Mon – June 8th – 6:00 – Court #1
8	vs.	2	Mon – June 8th – 6:00 – Court #2
6	vs.	4	Mon – June 8th – 8:00 – Court #1
1	vs.	5	Mon – June 8th – 8:00 – Court #2

Fifth Round

1	vs.	4	Wed – June 10th – 6:00 – Court #1
5	vs.	3	Wed – June 10th – 6:00 – Court #2
6	vs.	2	Wed – June 10th – 8:00 – Court #1
7	vs.	8	Wed – June 10th – 8:00 – Court #2

Sixth Round

1	vs.	3	Fri – June 12th – 6:00 – Court #1
4	vs.	2	Fri – June 12th – 6:00 – Court #2
5	vs.	8	Fri – June 12th – 8:00 – Court #1
6	vs.	7	Fri – June 12th – 8:00 – Court #2

Seventh Round

1	vs.	2	Mon – June 15th – 6:00 – Court #1
3	vs.	8	Mon – June 15th – 6:00 – Court #2
4	vs.	7	Mon – June 15th – 8:00 – Court #1
5	vs.	6	Mon – June 15th – 8:00 – Court #2

* The numbers in this round have been rearranged so that
Player #1 is scheduled at a later time and on a different
court than usual.

Figure 5-11. Sample round robin schedule for eight players.

ranking. A central listing of names and telephone numbers should also be posted at the tournament site. The ladder tournament may continue for an indefinite length of time.

Pyramid

The pyramid tournament is similar to the ladder format in that players may challenge other players to matches and competition may continue over a long period of time. Names of players are placed on rows of the pyramid by chance or by design. The pyramid may have any number of horizontal rows, depending on the number of participants. The bottom row, for example, might have six names on it. The next row above would have five names; the third row from the bottom, four names, etc. A player may challenge anyone on his row. The player who wins may then challenge a player on the row above. If the challenger wins that match, he changes places on the pyramid with the defeated player.

CONDUCTING CLINICS

Tennis clinics are usually held when a nationally or regionally known player or teacher is present to attract participants. However, any knowledgeable high school or college coach can direct a clinic for beginning, intermediate, and advanced players. A one day, do-it-yourself clinic can be an interest stimulator in the off-season, an event to begin a season, or a promotional idea any time of the year.

Many courts, instructors, and balls would be ideal for such a clinic, but an effective session can be conducted to accommodate up to one hundred participants with three courts, three coaches, instructors or advanced players, and three balls provided by each player who attends. Each of the three teachers should have at least one helper—preferably, but not necessarily, an experienced player.

Assuming that the clinic will be directed toward more than one age group, the natural divisions are adults, college age students, high school students, junior high school students, and a group for those in grades one through six. None of the groups should work more than an hour and a half, and if more than one age group is to be involved the same day, a time gap between sessions should be provided for in the schedule.

Regardless of the age or ability level of a group, a few major skills should be introduced, demonstrated, and practiced rather than attempting to cover every phase of the game in a short period of time. For beginners, the clinic will be successful if participants can learn a little about the forehand, backhand, punch serve, and how to keep score. For intermediate players, work on groundstrokes, the volley, and the serve is enough for one ninety-minute period. Tournament level players can be put through a brisk practice session for the same amount of time.

For the same reasons that relatively few skills should be practiced, relatively few teaching points should be emphasized. The objective of a one-shot clinic is to drive home a few ideas well, rather than to use the shotgun approach, hoping that a little bit of everything will hit everyone. Following are some suggestions regarding organization, drills, and teaching points to be emphasized for beginning, intermediate, and advanced groups:

Beginning Group

10 MINUTES—Explain and demonstrate the ready position, forehand grip, and footwork for the forehand stroke. Have the players line up in rows facing the instructor. The players follow the instructor's lead in a "Ready-Pivot-Step-Swing" drill. In the same formation, players can practice dribbling a ball against the court or in the air, using the correct forehand grip. This drill helps to develop ball control and also aids the beginner in establishing the hand to racket head distance relationship.

POINTS TO EMPHASIZE: 1) Keep the racket well up and in front of the body (pointing toward the net) in the ready position. 2) Pivot forward on every shot. 3) Make sure that the forehand grip allows the face to be perpendicular to the court as striking the ball is simulated.

---

20 MINUTES—Players line up on the opposite side of the net from the instructor's aides, who throw easy, waist high forehand shots. The instructor stands with those players doing the hitting. If aides are not available, players may be used as throwers. Those waiting to hit are used to retrieve balls.

POINTS TO EMPHASIZE: 1) Get the racket back on the backswing as the ball is thrown, not as it bounces. 2) Step into the ball. 3) Watch the ball leave the hitter's strings.

---

10 MINUTES—Explain and demonstrate the backhand grip and stroke. Repeat the "Ready-Pivot-Step-Swing" and dribbling drills, using backhand techniques.

POINTS TO EMPHASIZE: 1) Use the nonracket hand to guide the racket back on the backswing. 2) Pivot forward. 3) Follow through as if trying to slap the net with the back of the hand.

20 MINUTES—Have the aides throw backhand shots, employing the same procedure used in practicing the forehand.

POINTS TO EMPHASIZE: 1) Get the racket back early. 2) Use the opposite hand to aid in changing grips and to push the racket forward. 3) Strike the ball in front of the right foot (for righthanders).

10 MINUTES—Rest period. After the players get a drink of water, explain the fundamentals of scoring as they rest.

5 MINUTES—Explain and demonstrate the punch serve.

POINTS TO EMPHASIZE: 1) Grip the racket halfway between the Eastern and Western forehand grips. 2) Toss the ball in front of the body. 3) Toss the ball as high as the server can reach with the arm and racket extended.

15 MINUTES—Serving drill. Half of the group takes turns practicing the punch serve while the other half retrieves balls. Care should be taken to avoid having more than one person hitting at a time, and to see that balls are returned along the sides of the court so that the servers will not be interrupted.

POINTS TO EMPHASIZE: 1) Toss the ball without spin. 2) Contact with the ball is made with the arm fully extended, with the wrist flexing on contact. 3) Transfer the weight of the body forward as the serve is delivered.

Intermediate Group

30 MINUTES—Allow this much time to look at the group's groundstrokes. The throwing drill may have to be utilized, but having four players on one court at all times is preferable. If necessary, six players can fit onto one court for forehand and backhand practice. The players should be rotated frequently so that everyone gets plenty of action. Players not hitting should retrieve balls.

POINTS TO EMPHASIZE: 1) Be consistent in form and types of shots attempted. (Players at this stage frequently want to try everything, usually at the expense of further developing solid, consistent, basic strokes.) 2) Take an efficient, relatively short backswing. Big wind-ups are impractical. 3) Concentrate on keeping the ball in play.

30 MINUTES—Two-on-one volley drill. Two players alternately hit two balls each to a third player at the net. Use both sides of the court

if enough balls are available. Other players and aides pick up balls.

POINTS TO EMPHASIZE: 1) Bend at the knees and stay low. 2) Hit the ball before it gets even with you. The ball should be hit while it is still rising, not as it drops. 3) Use a Continental grip and take a short backswing.

---

30 MINUTES—Serving drill. Two players serve, two play the net, and two return serves. The instructor concentrates on the servers. Players rotate among all six positions.

POINTS TO EMPHASIZE: 1) Be consistent in tossing the ball prior to the serve. 2) Use a rhythmic, continuous motion in hitting the serve. 3) Place the ball at designated spots in the receiving court.

Advanced Group

30 MINUTES—Use a three shot, serve-rush-volley drill. The players serve alternately from the right and left sides. Servers follow the serve to the net. The player on the opposite side practices the service return by trying to pass his opponent. The server then attempts to volley that return. Play stops after three shots. Players rotate positions every five minutes. The instructor roams from a position behind the servers down the side of the court to the net.

POINTS TO EMPHASIZE: 1) Get set for the volley as the opponent strikes the ball, then make a secondary move for the volley. Rush behind the serve to establish a position in front of the service line before making the volley. 2) Hold the racket tightly on the volley and place the volley crosscourt to set up the opponent for the put-away shot. 3) Watch the opponent's racket head in order to anticipate where his return will be placed.

---

30 MINUTES—Two-on-one volley drill. Use the same procedure and points of emphasis as with the intermediate group.

---

15 MINUTES—"Quickie" drop shot games (doubles, if necessary). Score as usual. Only drops and angles are allowed. Everything beyond the service line is out.

POINTS TO EMPHASIZE: 1) Take the drill seriously. 2) Hit to open spots. 3) Disguise your shots.

---

15 MINUTES—Two-on-one overhead smash drill. The procedure is the

same as in the volley drill, except that those players at the baseline hit lobs.

POINTS TO EMPHASIZE: 1) Get the racket back quickly. 2) Take many short steps in preparing to hit. 3) Point to the ball with the nonracket hand for balance and position.[1]

SUPERVISING SUMMER PROGRAMS

Towns and cities throughout the country sponsor summer tennis programs consisting of supervised play, free or inexpensive group lessons, and tournaments. The purpose of these programs is usually consistent with a city recreation department concept of providing organized activities for large numbers of people.

Summer tennis programs last from two to three months, depending on when the public schools finish one academic year and begin another. These programs are funded through city or county governmental agencies, and the money is used to pay tennis directors and instructors, to maintain facilities, to buy supplies, and to purchase awards for city or regional tournaments. Smaller towns and cities may have programs completely organized and directed by one person. That person may be a fulltime employee of the city recreation department, but is more likely to be a school teacher, coach, college player, or some other person who is not otherwise employed during the summer months. In larger cities, the director may be allowed to hire parttime assistant instructors who are usually outstanding high school or college players in the area.

Starting a Program

There may be people in communities who are interested in starting an organized tennis program, but who are not sure about how to do it. Here are some suggestions. Call a meeting of five to ten people in the community who are interested in supporting or playing tennis and who are influential in business, education, or politics. This first meeting should not be a mass meeting of all persons interested in tennis; such a meeting may come later. The five to ten persons who come to the first meeting should try to establish the fact that there is a need for a program and then try to agree on the type of program they want. Once the basic program components have been agreed upon, the group should estimate

---

[1]Jim Brown, "Do-It-Yourself Tennis Clinic," *The Coaching Clinic*, 11, no. 1 (January, 1973) 9.

how much the program would cost and determine what personnel would be necessary to supervise activities. The steering committee might also discuss persons in the community who are qualified to be the program director and evaluate area tennis facilities in terms of organized activities.

With this information—type of program, cost, personnel needs, and facilities—the group is now ready to request a meeting with persons in city or county government. It is not necessary that the entire group attend this meeting, but it should be made clear that those attending represent the thinking of a larger number of people. The meeting held with government officials should be held as much as a year in advance of the proposed program because money will have already been budgeted for the current year. The group may not want to wait that long and it will do no harm to go ahead and make requests for a program during the year. However, for the best results, give the politicians time to allocate money for the program.

If possible, the tennis group should meet with the highest ranking governmental official in the community such as the mayor, president of the city council, or county commissioner. The city recreation director might be invited to attend, but the initial meeting should not be with him alone. He does not have the authority to install a program without the consent of higher authorities, and if he is working with a limited budget already, he is not likely to want another program of any type.

At the meeting, the spokesperson for the committee should state the purpose of the meeting and generally outline what the group has in mind in the way of a tennis program. When the mayor asks about costs, give him the figures your committee has established. If he asks about personnel to direct the program or about facilities, be ready to give the information your group has already discussed. Express any other opinions you have about the program, answer any further questions, and conclude the meeting. Before you leave, tell the officials that you realize that no decision can be made immediately, but that you would like to be notified if and when any action is taken. Be sure to volunteer the services of the group if help is needed in further discussions or in planning the program. Try to get some kind of commitment on when the next action on the proposal will be taken. That action could be a city council meeting in which your group should be represented.

After that meeting, there is not much you or your group can do except to follow up the meeting with a letter thanking the officials for their consideration and to seek the support of other politicians and residents of the community. The program will either be approved or rejected. If it is approved, further meetings may be necessary to organize activities or to discuss the program with the director. If the program is rejected, find out why, then reorganize for another meeting at a later date.

Whether the summer tennis program is a new one or one already in existence, it will probably consist of supervised play at city owned or operated courts, tennis instruction, and a series of tournaments. The remainder of this chapter contains ideas for the director of a program having any or all of those components.

Supervision

The city tennis director should realize that he or she is working with the public and be aware of what this means. First, it means that you are being paid by the city or county government and as such you are a member of the city's administrative team. You can complain to your supervisor about facilities, working conditions, or pay, but as far as the public is concerned, you are representing the interests of the city and should support these interests. Second, working with and for the public means that you are going to have to give up some of your privacy. People are going to call you at home at all hours to ask questions about the tennis program. You or your spouse can indignantly refer these callers to the city recreation department for information and alienate a potential tennis player or supporter, or you can politely give them the information requested and thank them for calling. If you want to look at the problem of home calls economically, consider the possibility that each call is a potential fifty to one hundred dollars in private tennis lessons (if you teach private lessons). Finally, working with the public means that you cannot please everybody. The most you can do is to go to work, do the best job you can, and try to get along with the people you see on the job. They will not all like the way you do your job, but you cannot let that disturb you to the point of worrying excessively or letting their criticism affect the way you do your job. You may be accused of favoritism, rigging the draw, being a poor teacher, and cheating on line calls during a junior tournament. Listen to the criticism; accept it if it is valid, and forget it if it is not. As long as you are honest with yourself about how you carry out your responsibilities and as long as the criticism is constructive, serving the public should be a pleasant experience.

Before the program activities begin, the director must spend some time preparing for the summer. These preparations include deciding on the general content of the program, preparing a schedule of events, hiring assistants, purchasing supplies, and publicizing the program. About two weeks before school is out, a news release should be prepared and distributed to newspapers, radio, and television stations. Here is a sample release:

The Lake Charles Recreation Department's annual summer tennis program will begin Monday, June 3rd, at three area tennis complexes.

Free tennis lessons for beginning players between the ages of eight and fifteen will be given at the Lake Charles High School courts from 8:00 to 9:00 am; at the McNeese courts from 9:15 to 10:15; and at Brentwood Park from 10:30 to 11:30. Participants must provide their own rackets and three marked tennis balls. The lessons will be taught five days a week for four weeks. Sessions for other age groups will be held later in the summer.

The courts at all three locations will be open to the public from 10:30 am until 11:00 pm daily. Reservations for court space may be made in advance by calling the Recreation Department office on Second Avenue.

In addition to lessons and supervised play, the city will sponsor a series of tournaments during July and August. Dates for those events will be announced later.

The summer tennis program will be directed by Jes Stewart. Stewart is a former varsity player at McNeese State University and is currently tennis coach at Marion High School.

Once the program begins, the director has some general supervisory responsibilities in addition to teaching lessons and directing competition. The most important of these responsibilities is to be present at the courts as much as possible and in particular during the peak hours of activity. In most communities, the hours of heavy tennis court use are between 5:00 and 9:00 pm. Priority should be given to adult players during those hours and to junior players earlier in the day. The director should be at the courts to record the names of players, to receive court use fees if there are any, to make court assignments, to enforce rules, and to generally see that the tennis traffic moves. If there are limits on the amount of time players may occupy a court, the director should notify players when the time period has expired. If there are no rules regarding the length of playing time, the supervisor should see that no one has to wait too long to get onto a court. This can be done by arranging doubles matches, setting up informal competition among players or teams, and diplomatically asking people who have been on the courts for a while to finish the set they are playing so that others can use the court. If the director records the names of players as they arrive at the courts, he not only has a record of court use, but he also gets to know people on a first name basis which will help when diplomatic requests for court space are necessary.

Some municipalities allow the director to teach private lessons on city courts during the time when he has no other specific responsibilities. This is a good policy because the director's salary is probably low and should be supplemented by pro shop receipts or lesson fees. However, the schedule of private lessons should not interfere with the primary part of the program, which is providing low cost supervised tennis activities for the public. If the director teaches private lessons, he should appoint someone to assume supervisory duties during that time.

As the program develops, the director will have to assume other responsibilities peculiar to his situation. Through his general supervision of the courts, he may be able to create interest in the other two phases of the summer program.

Instruction

Many summer programs begin with free group lessons for junior age players. These programs frequently begin the first Monday after the last day of school in May or June. If there is a time gap between the end of school and the beginning of tennis lessons, the children may become too involved in other activities to be interested in tennis. The lessons are usually given in the morning because the people in this age group are free at that time, and because there is not a big demand for use of the courts by adults.

Lessons may be given only at a central tennis center or they may be given at various locations throughout the city or county. Both systems have advantages and disadvantages. Tennis centers have many courts, and a large number of players can be supervised by a few instructors. It is also easy to keep tennis traffic moving at a large complex of courts. The disadvantage is that school age children may not be able to get transportation to take lessons or to play at a tennis center far from their homes. If the lessons are taught at neighborhood courts or schools, more children have access to program activities. However, either more instructors must be hired to teach and supervise at the various sites or the same few instructors have to move from place to place throughout the city during the day.

Group lessons last about an hour a day, two to five days a week, for a period of about four weeks. The hour long session is about as long as the younger players can concentrate on learning, as long as the instructors can teach one group effectively, and as long as the schedule of court use permits in many cities. The five-days-a-week schedule is preferable, but may not be possible if there are many groups to be taught. Four weeks of daily lessons is about the maximum length advisable. Many programs run for shorter periods. In the city recreation type of program, however, the children are going to be in and out because of vacations, ball games, and other summer activities. Very few participants will be there every day for a month. If there is a demand for more instruction, a new cycle of lessons can be started every three or four weeks.

Any experienced summer program director will testify that a lot of baby sitting goes on during free tennis lessons. Some of the kids want to be there and are enthusiastic about what is happening; others would just as soon be doing something else; and a third group is there because their parents dropped them off at the courts and told them to take lessons. It is difficult to plan a program of instruction for such a wide range of participants. As much as possible, separate the players by age groups and ability. Eight, nine, and ten year olds seem to get along with each other, eleven and twelve year olds stick together, and the thirteen to fifteen group should be separate from the younger players.

Mass instruction is mediocre at best, but there are some ways to make it worthwhile. Establish some basic goals of instruction like teaching everyone how to keep score and at least presenting the serve and groundstrokes to all players. There will be many juniors who can do much more, but there will also be some who cannot do that much. Use drills that keep everyone moving rather than standing in lines. The defection rate from tennis classes is highest where the lines are longest. Make effective use of lead-up games and activities for those who are not ready for actual tennis competition. Everybody there can achieve, even if it is just serving five balls in a row into the proper court. Give the learners something to work for—a ribbon, a certificate, or the opportunity to compete against each other or another park group in a tournament or match. Keep an eye open for talented players. In spite of all the disadvantages of public court group lessons, the real hungry players come out of that tennis environment. It is part of your job to recognize them, teach them, and give them an opportunity to develop their talents.

Municipal programs ought to provide group lessons for older adolescents and adults during the summer months. These lessons attract more people if they are taught late in the afternoon or at night when adults get off work. The exception to that suggestion may be lessons for housewives taught during the morning. The lessons should last for several weeks, but adults will not be able to attend daily as the juniors can. Two or three one hour sessions a week are enough, provided the participants get to practice on their own in addition to the classes.

Competition

City tennis tournaments are usually played during July or August. Junior events are held before adult competition and should culminate the program of instruction offered earlier in the summer. Children who have participated in the group lessons may constitute the bulk of the field for local junior events. In large cities, separate tournaments are held for each junior age division, beginning with the ten and under group and concluding with the eighteen and under division. Smaller towns may establish their own age group breakdowns, depending on the number of junior players in the program. The junior events should be scheduled during the day unless there is enough space and community interest to warrant occupying courts with junior competition at night. Be careful not to schedule city tournaments, whether they are for juniors or adults, when there will be a conflict with other major tournaments in the state. Many of the better players play in a state circuit and may miss their chances to be city champions if there is a schedule conflict. There should be little or no entry fee for a city sponsored junior tournament. In a recreation program, maximum participation is desirable, and charging entry fees will discourage maximum participation. The program is being financed by taxpayers anyway, so why charge them twice?

There are two ways to schedule the adult tournaments. One way is to conduct all singles and doubles play during a one-or two-week period of time. This method provides a great deal of concentrated activity, does not tie up the courts for long periods of time, and gives tennis a lot of newspaper space in a short period of time. Another way to schedule adult events is to space them out over a period of several weeks beginning in mid-July and finishing late in August. This method allows for a less concentrated, but more continuous form of competition. Participation is increased because players can enter in several divisions without worrying about tiring out as they would if every age group event were held the same week. Publicity is less splashy than it would be in one big tournament, but the continuous play ensures almost daily news stories about local tennis. Tournament matches must be held after working hours or on weekends, and local competition should not conflict with out of town tournaments. Again, entry fees should be very small if they are required at all. Some tournament directors require only that players bring a can of new tennis balls as an entry fee. A new can is opened for each match; the winner gets the unopened can; the loser gets to keep the used balls.

The most common divisions for adult competition are the open, the thirty-five and over category, and the forty-five and over group. Large cities may have divisions for players over fifty-five and players over sixty. In nonsanctioned tournaments, many communities have a tournament for players thirty and over and one for those forty and over instead of the traditional age divisions. Novice division tournaments for each age group have recently become popular. Leagues and ladders may also be put into the summer program of competition if time and court space permit.

DEVELOPING PROFESSIONALLY

Tennis teachers, coaches, and program directors can increase their knowledge of the sport and improve their instructional and administrative skills in many ways. There are national, regional, state, and local tennis organizations and organizations for physical educators and coaches. There are also tennis and coaching publications which contain tennis news, advertisements for products and services, and articles on teaching, coaching, and playing the game. Besides holding memberships in professional organizations and keeping up with tennis literature, tennis administrators can participate in many other activities which will help them to be more effective in their work.

Organizations

The United States Tennis Association is an organization open to any person interested in the game. Tennis players, officials, and supporters constitute the majority of members. The U.S.T.A. is involved in a variety of activities, including sanctioning of tournaments, conducting junior development programs, supporting Wightman Cup and Davis Cup teams, ranking players, and holding clinics for players, teachers, and coaches. The association's main office is in New York, and there are seventeen sections throughout the United States. Officials in each section promote and govern tournament competition in their area. Where a section encompasses more than one state, there may be state associations, also.

Members of the U.S.T.A. pay annual dues and receive a membership card which entitles them to participate in sanctioned tournaments; to be placed on the mailing list; to be ranked at the state, sectional, or national levels; and to receive *Tennis, USA,* a monthly magazine which is the organization's official publication.

A committee of the United States Tennis Association is the Tennis Umpires Association. It provides some sanctioned tournaments with umpires and linespersons who are qualified through training and experience. Members of this organization must pass a written and practical test. Members receive cards from the association and are entitled to present themselves or to be invited to any U.S.T.A. sanctioned tournament.

The United States Professional Tennis Association is an organization composed primarily of teaching professionals. There are fourteen

U.S.P.T.A. geographical sections in the country and members in almost every state. To become a member, a person must submit a membership application, successfully complete written and practical examinations covering material on tennis instruction, pro shop management, and administration of programs, and pay membership dues.

U.S.P.T.A. members are certified by the organization as teaching professionals; they receive the association's literature; they can attend the annual convention; and they may participate in individual and team tournaments held for members only. The U.S.P.T.A. has established an academy for the training of teaching professionals and there are plans for opening similar schools throughout the country.

The Intercollegiate Tennis Coaches Association consists of college and university tennis coaches. Members are required to pay annual dues. For their money, I.T.C.A. members receive a membership card, a newsletter which is published several times a year, and a tennis scorebook for team matches. The group holds two meetings a year—a winter meeting held in conjunction with the winter meeting of the National Collegiate Athletic Association, and a summer meeting conducted during the N.C.A.A. Division I tournament. This organization selects a twenty-four member All American tennis team every year, and the I.T.C.A. also makes recommendations to the N.C.A.A. regarding competition at the national tournament.

The American Alliance for Health, Physical Education, and Recreation is an organization with headquarters in Washington, D.C., and whose membership consists primarily of health and physical education teachers and athletic coaches. The organization is subdivided into regional and state divisions. Members can affiliate themselves with any of seven associations within the Alliance. Many tennis coaches belong to the National Association for Sport and Physical Education and to the National Association for Girls and Women in Sports, which are two of the seven associations. The A.A.H.P.E.R., N.A.S.P.E., and N.A.G.W.S. distribute literature, conduct research, promote physical fitness, sponsor conventions, conferences, and workshops, and cooperate with other organizations such as U.S.T.A. in advancing sport and physical education related activities.

Publications

Magazines containing tennis related material are usually directed toward one of three groups: tennis players and fans, tennis coaches and teachers, and persons with commercial tennis interests.

American Lawn Tennis, Racquets Canada, Tennis, Tennis Illustrated,

Tennis USA, Tennis World, and *World Tennis* are some of the more widely circulated magazines for players and fans. These publications have news stories, tournament results, features, editorial comments, columns, schedules for upcoming events, and instructional articles.

Athletic Journal, Coach and Athlete, Scholastic Coach, and *The Coaching Clinic* are not tennis magazines, but are general coaching magazines which have articles related to tennis teaching and coaching. These articles usually appear in issues published during the January to June period. The *Journal of Health, Physical Education and Recreation* occasionally has articles related to tennis.

Tennis Industry and *Tennis Trade* are tennis business magazines, and have information for the teaching professional, pro shop operator, and tennis club manager. The articles are specifically written to help the professional become a better teacher and to be a more effective businessperson. *Tennis Gazette* is directed to managers of clubs and shops as well as to tennis players.

It would be difficult to list all of the books which might be helpful to tennis teachers, coaches, and program directors. Here are a few names of authors and the books they have written:

ANNARINO, ANTHONY, *Tennis Individualized Instructional Program*
BARNABY, JOHN, *Racket Work: The Key to Tennis*
DRIVER, HELEN, *Tennis for Teachers*
FAULKNER, EDWIN, AND WEYMULLER, FREDERICK, *Tennis: How to Play It, How to Teach It*
GOULD, DICK, *Tennis, Anyone?*
JAEGER, ELOISE, AND LEIGHTON, HARRY, *Teaching Of Tennis*
JOHNSON, JOAN, AND XANTHOS, PAUL, *Tennis*
KRAFT, EVE, *A Teacher's Guide to Group Tennis Instruction*
KRAFT, EVE, *The Tennis Workbook*
KENFIELD, JOHN, *Teaching and Coaching Tennis*
LEIGHTON, JIM, *Inside Tennis*
MASON, ELAINE, *Tennis*
MURPHY, BILL, AND MURPHY, CHET, *Tennis for the Player, Teacher and Coach*
TILMANIS, GUNDARS, *Advanced Tennis for Coaches, Teachers and Players*

Tennis Activities

Here is a list of ways in which a person interested in teaching, coaching, or directing tennis programs might further develop his or her professional skill and knowledge:

1. Join or organize local tennis associations or groups which promote tennis, hold clinics, and conduct competition.

2. Participate in or observe local, state, regional, and national tournaments.
3. Attend tennis camps.
4. Take private or group lessons.
5. Attend workshops, clinics, and conferences for teachers and coaches.
6. Become active in the U.S.T.A. by serving on committees or running for offices.
7. Join booster groups for high school and college teams.
8. Write and submit articles for publication in tennis magazines.
9. Play tennis regularly for fun and fitness.

6 Drills

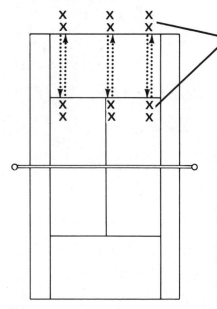

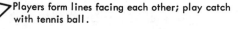
Players form lines facing each other; play catch with tennis ball.

Figure 6-1.

1. Baseball Throw (Beginners—Two to Twenty Players)

This drill is simply a game of catch with a tennis ball. Beginning players line up in two or more groups facing each other or facing the teacher at a distance of about twenty feet. Each player throws to another in an overhand motion, then goes to the end of the line. The teacher observes each player, and makes necessary corrections in the throwing motion. The better the form in throwing, the easier the serve will be to learn. The two motions are almost the same.

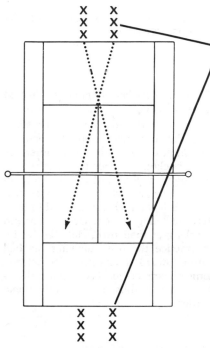

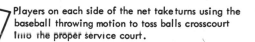

Players on each side of the net take turns using the baseball throwing motion to toss balls crosscourt Into the proper service court.

Figure 6-2.

2. Throw Into Service Court (Beginners —Two to Twenty Players)

To follow up the baseball throw drill, the players are positioned behind the service line or behind the baseline. The drill consists of using the baseball throwing motion to throw the tennis ball into the proper service court. Players may rotate after every throw or series of throws. When all of the balls have been retrieved by players on the opposite side of the net, these players return the balls by throwing them into the proper court.

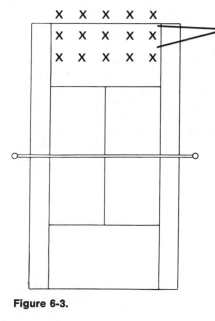

Players spread out; face same direction; practice service toss.

Figure 6-3.

3. Toss and Catch (Beginners—Two to Twenty Players)

Players are positioned anywhere on the court, but facing the same direction and with enough space to move freely. Either on signal or working individually, each player goes through the preliminary service motion, but catches the toss instead of continuing the motion. The purpose of the drill is to practice the toss. The instructor moves through the group as the toss is practiced.

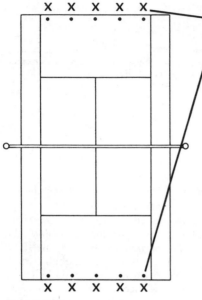

Players practice the service toss by allowing the ball to drop into a target.

Figure 6-4.

4. Toss Into Basket (Beginners—Two to Twenty Players)

Players are stationed along the baseline, facing the net, with enough room to avoid interfering with each other. A basket, bucket, or other target is placed on the court slightly in front of the baseline in a position where the service toss would fall if the ball was allowed to drop instead of being served. On a command or working at their own pace, the beginners practice the toss, allowing the ball to drop toward the target. Competition among players or goals for each individual may be established for motivational purposes.

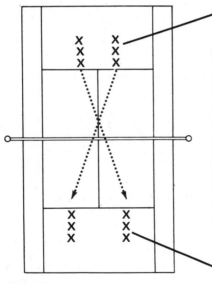

Players serve from half court.

Players in these lines retrieve balls.

Figure 6-5.

5. Half Court Serve (Beginners—Two to Twenty Players)

Beginners, especially those in the ten and under age group, practice the serve from a position behind the service line. One, two, three, or four lines may be formed, and each player gets at least two practice serves before rotating. Half of the group serves while the other half lines up in the same formation on the other side of the net to retrieve balls. As players' skills improve, serving positions are progressively moved toward the baseline.

6. Serve Into Fence (Beginners—Two to Forty Players)

If groups are too large for the available space, or if the number of balls does not allow for actual serving practice, have the players face the fences or walls surrounding the court at a distance of ten to twelve feet. The players serve into the fence as the instructor moves through the group to observe and correct swings. Allow for adequate space between the players to avoid accidents.

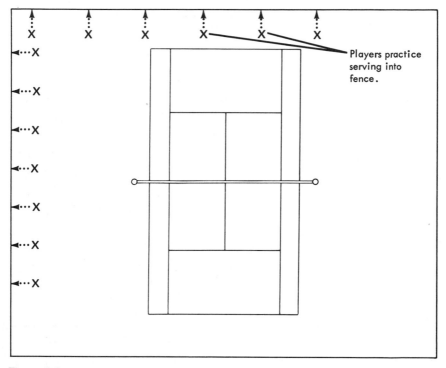

Players practice serving into fence.

Figure 6-6.

7. Suspended Ball (Beginners—Two to Four Players)

A tennis ball is attached to a length of cord, wire, or string, and suspended from a ceiling or from an apparatus extending out from a fence. The ball should be suspended at a point where contact should be made on the serve, and it should be possible to adjust the height of the ball according to the player's height and reach. Players practice the service motion and hit the suspended ball at the proper height. Several players can participate in the drill simultaneously if there are enough suspended balls, but the teacher should be in a position to observe and make corrections when necessary.

8. Serve From Fence *(Intermediates and Advanced—Two to Eight Players)*
In order to overload the muscles used in the serve, the players practice serving
from a position well behind the baseline or from the fence. After practicing
the serve from this distance over a period of time, the player should have
more power from the normal serving position.

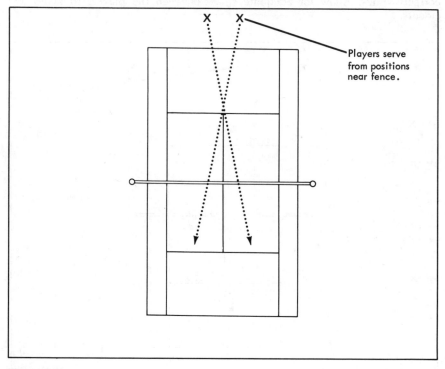

Players serve
from positions
near fence.

Figure 6-7.

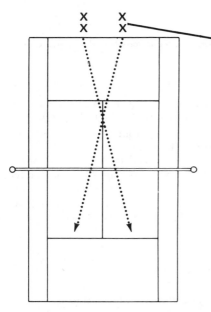

Players serve from the baseline with one knee on the court. This position forces the server to use topspin.

Figure 6-8.

9. One Knee Serve (Intermediates and Advanced—One to Four Players)

In order to develop the technique of putting topspin on the serve, players get down on one knee and serve from a position behind the baseline. The low position of the racket at the peak of the swing forces the server to put topspin on the ball in order for it to clear the net and fall into the service court.

10. Deep, Topspin Serve (Advanced—Two to Eight Players)

Place a temporary net or wall beside the regular net. The temporary net should be at least twice the height of the regulation net. Players must serve over the temporary net, using an exaggerated topspin action. The server should also place the ball deeply into the opponent's service court. Overlearning the topspin serve will help on second serve situations, in doubles competition, and when the server needs time to follow his serve to the net.

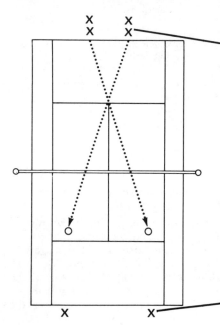

Players serve to targets in the service court.

11. Serve to Targets *(Intermediates and Advanced—Two to Eight Players)*

Players serve from singles or doubles positions to specific areas of the court which are marked by tennis ball cans or racket covers. The servers should alternate sides regularly. Others in the practice group practice returning, but the action stops after two shots—the serve and the return.

Players practice the return of serve.

Figure 6-9.

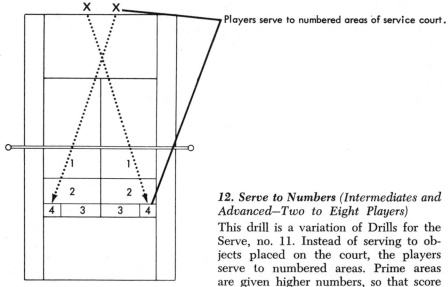

Players serve to numbered areas of service court.

12. Serve to Numbers *(Intermediates and Advanced—Two to Eight Players)*

This drill is a variation of Drills for the Serve, no. 11. Instead of serving to objects placed on the court, the players serve to numbered areas. Prime areas are given higher numbers, so that score may be kept for intrateam competition.

Figure 6-10.

DRILLS FOR GROUNDSTROKES

1. Ups and Downs (Beginners—Two to Twenty Players)
Players hold their rackets with the Eastern forehand grip and dribble a tennis ball against the court. Goals of 25, 50, or 100 "downs" may be used to stimulate interest. Players then turn the palm up and practice air dribbles or "ups." Variation: *Shadow Downs*. In this drill, "downs" are practiced, but a second ball is placed on the court. Players attempt to dribble one ball on the shadow of the second ball.

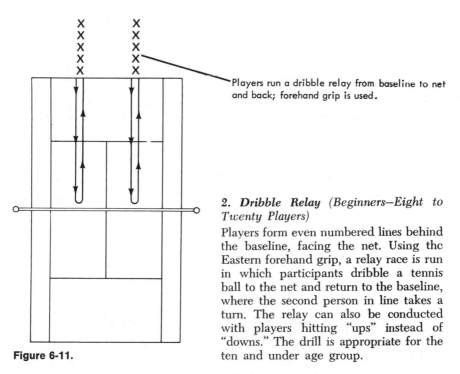

Players run a dribble relay from baseline to net and back; forehand grip is used.

2. Dribble Relay (Beginners—Eight to Twenty Players)

Players form even numbered lines behind the baseline, facing the net. Using the Eastern forehand grip, a relay race is run in which participants dribble a tennis ball to the net and return to the baseline, where the second person in line takes a turn. The relay can also be conducted with players hitting "ups" instead of "downs." The drill is appropriate for the ten and under age group.

Figure 6-11.

3. Progression Drill (Beginners—Two to Twenty Players)
This is a series of drills leading to the forehand stroke. Step #1: The player drops a ball and catches it with the other hand, using a forehand swing motion. Step #2: The player drops the ball and hits it with an open hand to a partner or to the teacher. Step #3: The player drops the ball and hits it with a forehand stroke, choking up on a racket. Step #4: The player drops the ball and hits it with a forehand stroke, holding the racket at the grip.

4. Footprints (Beginners—Two to Ten Players)
The instructor prepares paper outlines of feet. The outlines are placed in positions to indicate where the feet should be moved in preparing to hit a

forehand or backhand shot. The players then simulate the movement necessary to hit those shots, stepping on the paper outlines. At first, the drill may be performed individually in order for the beginners to become accustomed to the pattern of movement. Then the entire group may follow the lead of the instructor in practicing the footwork.

5. Ready, Pivot, Step, Swing *(Beginners—Two to Twenty Players)*

This is a footwork drill to be directed by the teacher, who faces the group. The instructor either says the words: Ready, Pivot, Step, and Swing, or One, Two, Three, Four. The players assume the ready position on the "Ready" command; pivot so that the side is to the net on the word "Pivot;" step forward slightly (into the ball) on "Step;" and go through with the swing on the last command. Although this drill is effective with beginners of almost any age, the instructor should be careful not to teach a mechanical, stiff preparation for groundstrokes. Once the concept of preparation is learned, the drill should be modified to include movements to either side of the court.

6. Toss to Forehand *(Beginners—Two to Ten Players)*

The title explains the drill. The instructor tosses soft bouncers to the forehand side of the student. The student practices preparation and stroking the ball, aiming for the teacher. If large groups are involved, players find a partner, spread out on the court, and take turns tossing and hitting. Some students may be used to retrieve balls. Competition can consist of the total number of balls hit into the proper area by two or more groups.

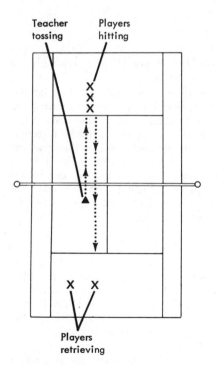

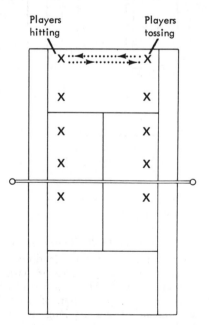

Figure 6-12a.   **Figure 6-12b.**

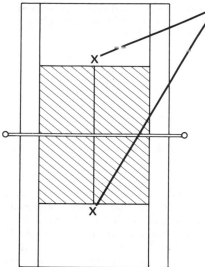

Players play regular games, but ball must be hit into area marked by diagonal lines.

Figure 6-13.

7. Short Game (Intermediates and Advanced—Two, Three, or Four Players)

Participants play singles, doubles, or two against one, but with these rules: 1) the normal service lines become baselines; 2) serve by dropping the ball and putting it into play; 3) volleys and smashes are illegal. Emphasis is on ball control, angles, and dropshots.

8a. Wall Strokes (Intermediates and Advanced—One or Two Players)
A player practices forehand and backhand strokes by hitting against a wall or backboard. The player should stand at a distance from the wall comparable to the distance from the baseline to the net. Shots should be directed to a point over a line on the wall indicating the height of a net.
8b. Alternating Wall Strokes. Two players alternate hitting groundstrokes against the wall, counting the number of consecutive hits or competing against each other by counting the number of misses.

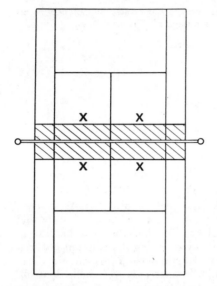

Figure 6-14.

Players compete against each other, keeping score as usual, but only shots falling into the marked area are in play.

9. Drop Shot Game (Intermediates and Advanced—Two to Four Players)

The players play games as in the "Short Game" drill, but now no shots may land beyond a chalk line approximately six feet from and parallel to the net. Two, three, or four players may compete. If there is an odd number of players, they should rotate so that each person gets the oportunity to play alone against the other two.

10. Slow Point Game (Intermediates and Advanced—Two to Four Players)

Two, three, or four players play regular games, but only groundstrokes may be used. Serves are put into play by dropping the ball and hitting it into the proper service court. Groundstrokes may be placed, but the idea is to keep the ball in play until someone makes an error rather than putting shots away. Players may not hit volleys or overhead smashes.

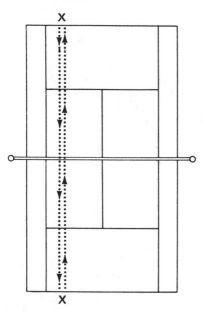

Figure 6-15.

Players warmup by hitting groundstrokes down the line; change sides after 5-10 minutes.

11. Down-the-Line Warmup (Advanced —Two Players)

Two players on opposite ends of the court move slightly to one side of the center mark. The ball is put into play, and the players hit all shots down the line on that side of the court. All shots should be played on one bounce. After hitting down the line for five to ten minutes, the players change sides (not ends), hitting down the opposite side lines for the same time period.

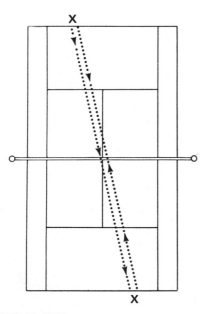

Figure 6-16.

Players use 5-10 minute warmup hitting crosscourt groundstrokes.

12. One-on-One Crosscourt (Advanced— Two Players)

Two players line up on opposite ends of the court in positions to warm up with crosscourt groundstrokes. Shots should be placed deeply, crosscourt, and played on the first bounce. The players should change sides after five minutes.

13. Two-on-One Crosscourt (Advanced—Three Players)

Players A and B take positions on the same baseline. Player C takes a position on the opposite side of the net behind an alley. A puts the ball in play down the line. C responds with a crosscourt shot, and moves along his baseline to prepare for another crosscourt shot. B returns the first crosscourt shot with another down-the-line placement, which is returned again by Player C. A and B will remain in their respective areas; C will move from side to side. Each player should get a five minute turn at each position.

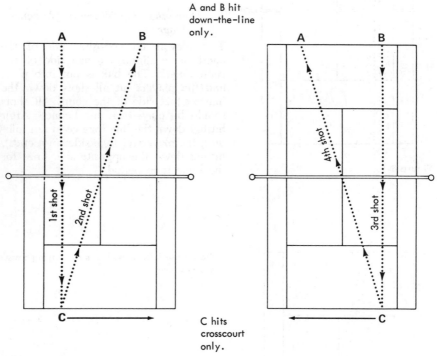

Figure 6-17a.　　　　　　　　　　　　　　　　**Figure 6-17b.**

14. Down-the-Line Crosscourt Combination *(Advanced—Two Players)*

One player puts the ball into play, hitting down the line. After he hits, he moves to the opposite side of the court to prepare to hit a second down-the-line shot. This player will continue to hit all shots down the line as long as the ball is in play. On receiving the first shot, a second player hits his groundstroke crosscourt, then moves to the opposite side to prepare to hit another. The second player will hit only crosscourt shots. If the players can keep the ball in play, the drill should last at least five minutes.

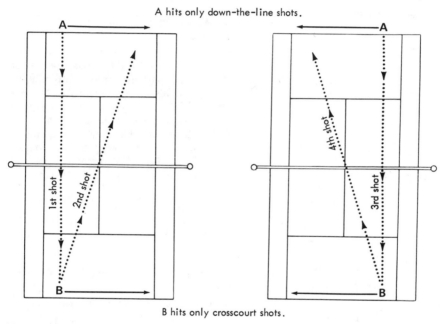

A hits only down-the-line shots.

B hits only crosscourt shots.

Figure 6-18a.   **Figure 6-18b.**

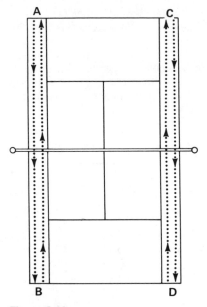

Figure 6-19.

A vs. B and C vs. D practice groundstrokes by hitting to alleys.

15. Alleys Only (Advanced—Two Players per Alley)

Players take positions on opposite ends of the court behind the baseline. After putting the ball into play, both players attempt to hit all groundstrokes so that they fall into the opponent's alley. Score may be kept by counting the number of shots falling into the alley. For example, the first player to score twenty points wins the game. The remainder of the court may be used by other players.

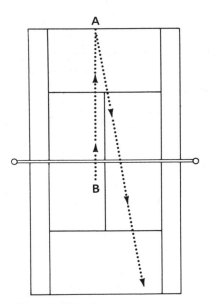

Figure 6-20.

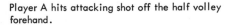

Player A hits attacking shot off the half volley forehand.

Player B or coach drives shots at feet of Player A.

16. Half Volley Attack (Advanced—Two Players)

The tournament tennis player must learn to turn the deeply hit half volley into an attacking shot of his own. The coach stands at the net with a basket of balls, and drives shots at the player's feet. The player stands on the baseline, steps into every shot driven at him, and half volleys a forehand. The purpose is to condition the player to make attacking shots out of what are normally defensive shots.

17. Set Up Approach Shots (Advanced—Two to Six Players)

The coach or an advanced player takes a position behind the baseline and near one alley. Players line up near the baseline on the other side of the net. Following a brief rally, the first player is set up with a short shot to one side of the court. The player advances and executes a down-the-line approach shot. By using a basket of balls, several players can get into the rotation, advancing, hitting, and returning to the end of the line. The drill can be expanded to simulate complete points.

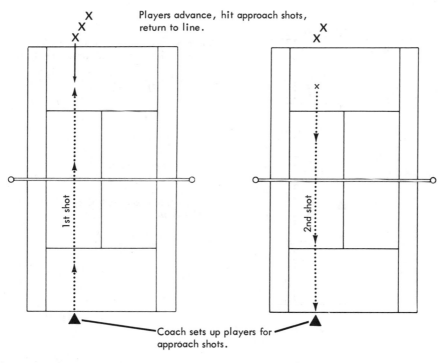

Figure 6-21a.   **Figure 6-21b.**

18. Running Groundstrokes (Advanced—Two Players)

The coach stands in the forecourt with a basket of balls, and the player starts the drill standing in the middle of the opposite court at the baseline. The coach alternately hits balls to each corner of the singles court, forcing the player to hit forehand and backhand groundstroke returns while running. At least 25 and as many as 100 balls can be hit consecutively, depending on the physical condition of the player. Although only one player at a time may participate in the drill, a second player can be used to retrieve balls and take a turn hitting while the first player rests.

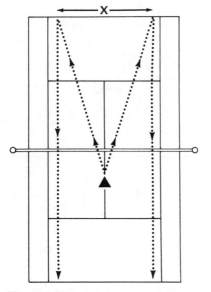

Player moves alternately to each corner, hitting forehand and backhand ground strokes.

Coach hits or throws balls to corners of the singles court.

Figure 6-22.

DRILLS FOR THE VOLLEY

1. Reach and Catch (Beginners—One to Four Players)
This drill can be used as the first step in the progression for teaching the volley to beginners. The player stands near the net in the ready position. The teacher stands on the opposite side of the net and either tosses or softly hits shots to either side of the player. The player reaches out and "catches" or stops the ball with the racket. Although no attempt is made to actually make a return volley, some balls may cross the net. Once the beginner can consistently stop the ball with the racket strings, the teacher can begin to teach the volleying motion.

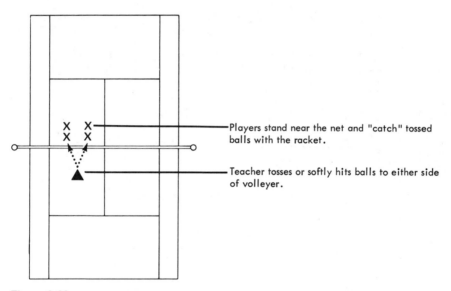

Players stand near the net and "catch" tossed balls with the racket.

Teacher tosses or softly hits balls to either side of volleyer.

Figure 6-23.

2. Toss to Volley (Beginners—Two to Ten Players)

The instructor tosses or hits balls to the player standing two or three steps from the net. Instead of just stopping the ball with the racket as in the *Reach and Catch* drill, the beginner volleys the ball in the direction of the teacher. If large groups are being taught, the partner method of tossing and volleying may be used. After the forehand volley is practiced, balls should be tossed to the backhand side. As the student becomes more comfortable at the net, balls may be tossed or hit to either side of the player.

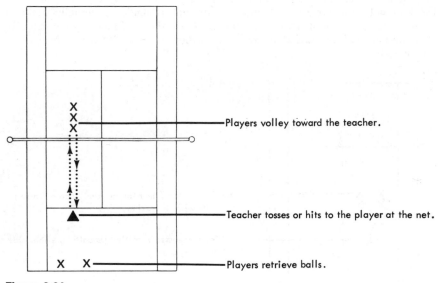

Players volley toward the teacher.

Teacher tosses or hits to the player at the net.

Players retrieve balls.

Figure 6-24.

3. Volley From Fence *(Beginners and Intermediates—Two to Twenty Players)*
In order to teach the short backswing required for volleys, the player is positioned with his back near the fence or wall surrounding the court. The instructor hits or tosses balls, and the player is forced to return with a short backswing volley. If the group is large, players may be paired so that each has one turn tossing and one turn volleying.

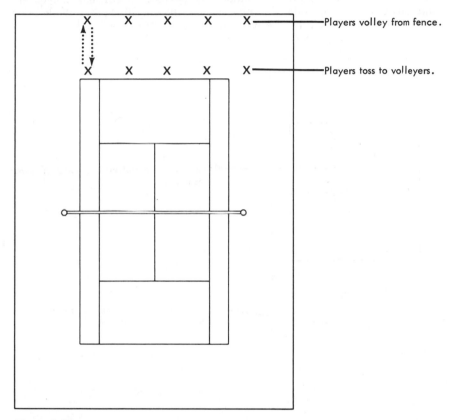

Figure 6-25.

4. Volley From Gate *(Beginners and Intermediates—Two to Six Players)*
In order to teach the short backswing and the forward motion necessary for volleys, the player is positioned in the space normally occupied by a closed gate. The coach hits or tosses balls, and the player is forced to step forward, using a short backswing to volley the ball. If he touches the fence with the racket, he is either not stepping forward or taking too long a backswing.

5. *Crosscourt Set-ups* *(Beginners and Intermediates—Two to Eight Players)*
As the player learns when to come to the net and how to hit the volley, he
can begin to place the ball to various spots on the court. In this drill, the
instructor hits medium paced shots down the line to the player at the net,
who volleys the ball crosscourt to the open area. The drill should be repeated
on the opposite side of the court so the player can practice forehand and
backhand crosscourt volleys. A rotation can be used in which a player hits
and moves to the other side of the court or to the end of the line while other
players move into the volleying position.

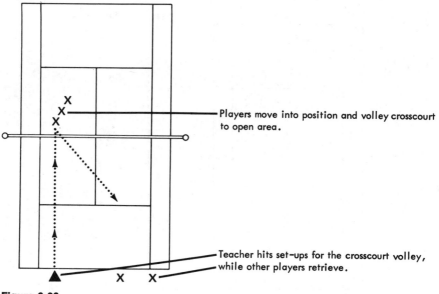

Players move into position and volley crosscourt to open area.

Teacher hits set-ups for the crosscourt volley, while other players retrieve.

Figure 6-26.

6. *Umpiring Drill* *(Intermediates and Advanced—One or Two Players)*
Some players have difficulty in knowing which shots are going in and which
ones are going to be out. Misjudgment frequently occurs when high, hard
shots are hit toward a man at the net. In this drill, a coach or advanced player
has a basket of balls and stands on one baseline. A second player is positioned
in an area where he would normally hit volleys. The coach hits shots in his
direction, but rather than volleying, the player at net simply calls balls "in"
or "out" before they hit the court. Each team member gets the same number
of calls if score is kept.

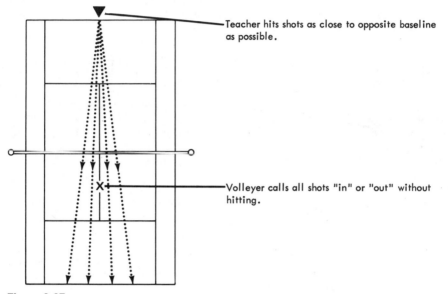

Teacher hits shots as close to opposite baseline
as possible.

Volleyer calls all shots "in" or "out" without
hitting.

Figure 6-27.

7. *Wall Volley* *(Advanced—One or Two Players)*
In this drill, a player counts the number of times he can volley against a wall
or board without missing. To stimulate team competition, each player's score
is recorded and compared to others. Variation: *Alternating Wall Volley.* Two
players alternate hitting volleys against a wall. Competition may be between
the two players or between two-player teams.

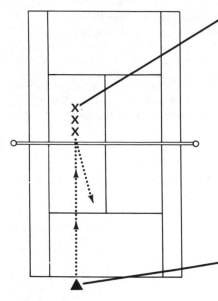

Players volley shots hit close to the top of the net.

8. Net Skimmers (Intermediates—Two to Eight Players)

This is another drill in which the instructor hits shots to a player at the net, but the emphasis is on returning balls that skim over the top of the net. The volleyer must bend the knees to get down to eye level with the ball and concentrate on keeping the ball in play rather than making a forcing return.

Instructor hits shots as close to the top of the net as possible.

Figure 6-28.

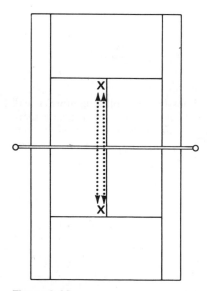

Players put a ball into play and count the number of consecutive volleys hit.

9. Counting Volleys (Intermediates—Two Players)

Two players stand on opposite sides of the net in deep volleying positions. A ball is put into play and the players count the number of consecutive volleys hit. Team or individual records may be established to stimulate interest in the drill. Doubles teams may also compete against each other, but the emphasis is on keeping the ball in play rather than hitting winners.

Figure 6-29.

10. Volley Through the Ring *(Advanced—Two Players)*

A ring or hoop is mounted and placed two to three feet above the net. Two players attempt to volley through the ring, practicing ball control volleys. Score may be kept between individuals or doubles teams. The players may line up directly opposite each other or at crosscourt angles.

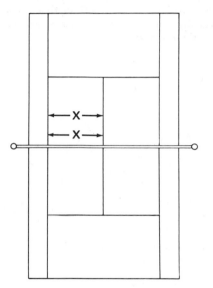

Figure 6-30.

Players move from center line to sideline touching racket to court ten or more times.

11. Side-to-Side *(Advanced—One to Six Players)*

The player stands in a volleying position near the net, halfway between the center line and the singles sideline. When given a signal, he moves laterally as fast as possible to the right, touches the singles sideline with the racket, then moves to the left and touches the center line with the racket. He completes ten touches (or any number determined by the teacher or coach) before stopping. Several players can do the drill simultaneously by forming a line parallel to the sideline behind the first player. The drill is effective for conditioning and for improving lateral mobility.

12. Two-on-One Volley *(Intermediates and Advanced—Three Players)*

Two players are positioned near a basket of balls on the baseline. A third player takes a position across the net ready to hit volleys. The baseline players alternate hitting two balls each to the net man in a rapid-fire type drill. No attempt is made to return the volleys. The players rotate after each basket of balls. Other players may be used to pick up balls. Variation: *Two-on-One Volley Rally.* With tournament players, the drill may be varied so that balls are kept in play as long as possible. The baseline players practice groundstrokes and passing shots, while the net player works on deep volleys.

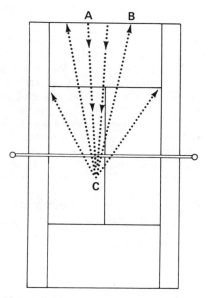

Players A and B feed Player C with groundstrokes.

Player C puts away volleys.

Figure 6-31.

13. Halfcourt One-on-One (Advanced—Two Players)

One player stands at the net halfway between the center line and the singles sideline. Another player stands at the opposite baseline between the same two lines. A ball is put into play; beginning with the third shot, the player on the baseline tries to pass the player at the net, who defends the halfcourt area in which he is standing. Shots which land beyond the halfcourt boundaries described are out. Score can be kept by counting the number of misses or by keeping score as in a regular game.

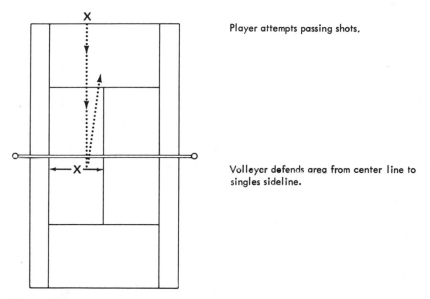

Player attempts passing shots.

Volleyer defends area from center line to singles sideline.

Figure 6-32.

14. Advancing Volleys (Advanced—Two Players)

Two players stand on opposite ends of the court facing each other. A ball is put into play. With each shot that is hit the player who hits the shot moves one step forward until players are firing at almost point blank range. When a shot is missed, both players must return to the baseline. The drill begins as a groundstroke drill, but as the players move toward the net, it becomes a volley drill.

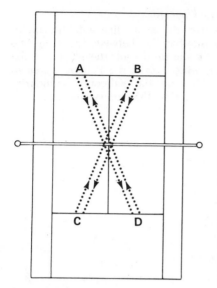

Figure 6-33.

Players A vs. D and B vs. C keep crosscourt volleys in play as long as possible.

15. Crosscourt Volleys (Advanced—Two or Four Players)

Two or four players take positions just behind the service lines opposite each other in crosscourt alignments. The players practice crosscourt volleys by keeping the ball in play as long as possible. Score may be kept. The players should change positions periodically. The drill may be conducted with four players by keeping two balls in play simultaneously.

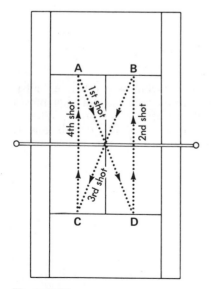

Figure 6-34.

Players keep volleys in play; A to D to B to C to A, etc.

16. Alternating Volleys (Advanced—Four Players)

Four players take positions just behind the service lines opposite each other in crosscourt alignments. The players practice volleys, but must hit in this order: Player A to Player D to Player B to Player C, back to Player A, etc. The order in which volleys are hit should be changed frequently so that the players practice volleying in different directions.

17. Know Your Partner (Intermediates and Advanced—Two Players)
In order for new doubles partners to get to know each other's moves, range, and capabilities, place the partners in volleying positions. A third person drives shots down the middle of the court within the reach of both players. The partners must learn to react not only to the shot, but to what his partner will do in a given situation.

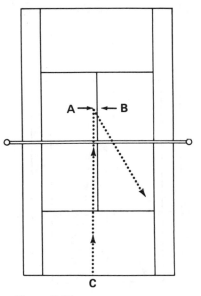

Doubles partners volley shots hit down the middle.

C drives shots down the middle of the court.

Figure 6-35.

COMBINATION DRILLS

1. Serve, Rush, and Volley (*Advanced—Two to Eight Players*)

This is a three shot drill. Player A serves and rushes the net, Player B returns the serve, and Player A hits a crosscourt volley. The same drill can be structured for doubles situations by adding a net player, a receiver's partner, and moving the server closer to the alley.

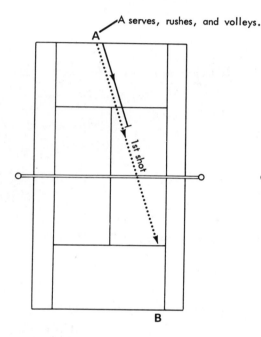

Figure 6-36a.

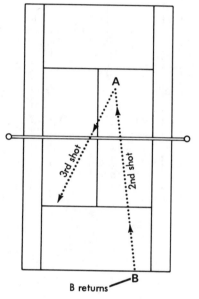

Figure 6-36b.

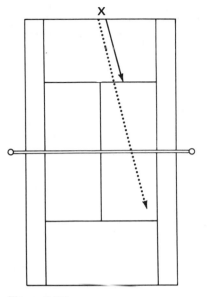

Figure 6-37.

Player serves and moves to a volleying position while coach times his approach to that position.

2. Stop Watch Drill *(Advanced—Two to Eight Players)*

This drill is a variation of the *Serve, Rush, and Volley* drill. The player serves and moves in to a volleying position. The coach records the time it takes for the server to reach the volleying position. The purpose of the drill is to make the player conscious of getting good court position, but this should not be done at the expense of losing body control. The velocity of the serve must also be taken into account; fast serves give the server less time to rush, while slow serves give him more time.

3. Approach and Volley (Intermediates and Advanced—Two to Eight Players)

The player takes a position in the middle of the court at the baseline. The teacher or coach hits shots that fall short enough on either side of the singles court so that the player can move in to hit the down-the-line approach shot. After that shot is hit, the instructor returns the ball with a down-the-same-line set-up which the attacking player puts away with a crosscourt volley. The drill should be executed on both sides so the player gets practice hitting forehand and backhand approach shots and volleys.

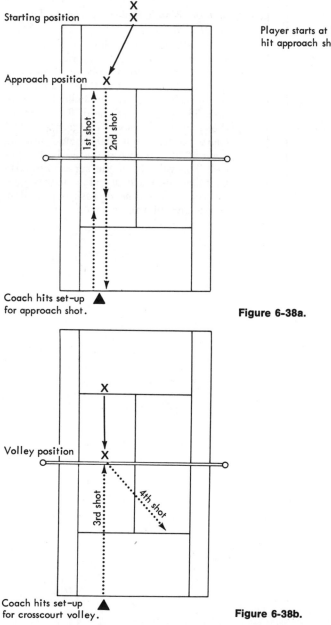

Player starts at baseline; moves in to hit approach shot and volley.

Figure 6-38a.

Figure 6-38b.

4. Serve, Approach, and Volley *(Intermediates and Advanced—Two to Eight Players)*

This drill is an extension of the drill previously described (Figure 6-38). Instead of beginning with an approach set-up by the coach, the player serves the ball. The complete sequence is: 1) player serves; 2) coach returns with an approach set-up; 3) player hits down-the-line approach shot; 4) coach returns down the same line; 5) player hits crosscourt volley.

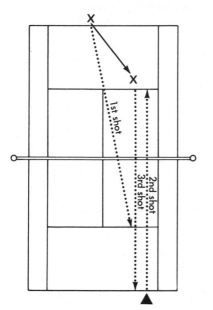

Player serves.

Hits approach shot.

Coach returns serve, hits set-ups for approach.

Figure 6-39a.

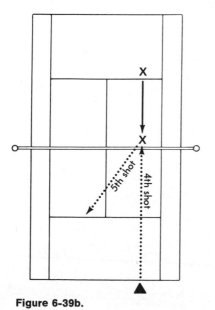

Follows approach shot to net.

Hits crosscourt volley.

Coach returns approach shot with set-up for volley.

Figure 6-39b.

5. Service Return Attack *(Intermediates and Advanced—Two Players)*

Two players play games or sets, but the server is not allowed to come to the net following the serve. The player returning the serve attempts to hit forcing returns so that he can take the net. After the first two shots, either player may move in to a volleying position. The purpose of the drill is to develop a player's ability to hit forcing shots against a nonattacking server.

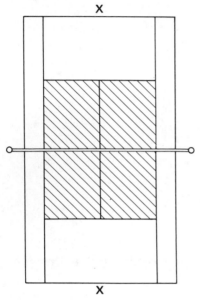

Players hit groundstrokes until one shot falls into marked area; opponent responds with approach shot; point is played out.

Figure 6-40.

6. Attack *(Advanced—Two, Three, or Four Players)*

Two players begin hitting groundstrokes from baseline positions. When either player hits a shot which falls into the opponent's service court area, the opponent responds with an approach shot, and rushes the net. From that position, the point is played out under game conditions.

7. *Get to the Net (Advanced—Four Players)*

Two doubles teams play a twenty-one point game. The serve changes every time the score equals a multiple of five. A team that wins an exchange when both partners have taken a position inside the service line receives two points. If either partner is behind the service line, only one point is earned. The purpose of this drill is to stimulate doubles partners to attack and take positions at the net.

8. *Receiver's Advantage (Intermediates and Advanced—Two or Four Players)*

Players or doubles teams play five-point games. However, the server or serving team gets only one-half point on each exchange won while the receiving player or team gets one point. The difference offsets the advantage usually held by the server.

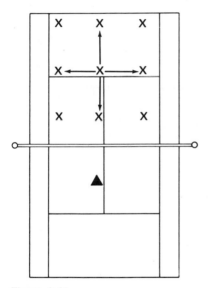

Players move in the direction indicated by the coach.

Coach motions, indicating forward, backward or lateral movement.

9. *Wave Drill (Beginners, Intermediates, Advanced—Two to Twenty Players)*

This is a footwork drill in which players are positioned in rows, facing the net, with room to maneuver. The instructor indicates either forward, backward, or lateral movement by waving his hand. As he motions, the players move in the direction indicated, and they carry their rackets as if preparing to hit a shot. The drill may be used to develop footwork and as a conditioning drill.

Figure 6-41.

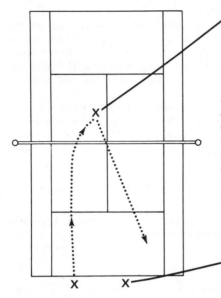

Player practices the overhead smash.

10. Lob and Smash (Intermediates and Advanced—Two to Four Players)

One or two players alternate hitting lobs while one or two others practice hitting overhead smashes. The drill may consist of only two or three shots, or may continue as long as the players hitting lobs can retrieve and return shots.

Players lob to opponent at net and attempt to retrieve smashes.

Figure 6-42.

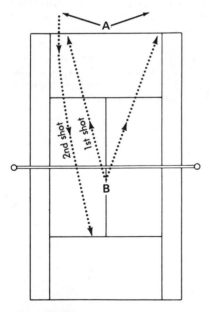

Player A retrieves deep drives; returns with high, deep, defensive lob.

Player B or coach drives shots deeply to either forehand or backhand.

11. Defensive Lobs (Advanced—Two to Six Players)

The coach or teacher stands at the net with a basket of balls. The player assumes a position in the middle of the baseline on the opposite side of the net. The coach drives shots deep to either corner, and the player attempts to chase the shots down, return shots with a high, deep, defensive lob, and return to a central position on the baseline. This drill consists of only two shots.

Figure 6-43.

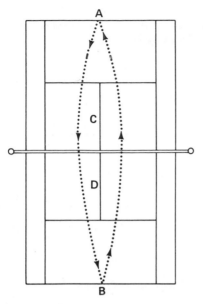

Figure 6-44.

Players A and B hit lobs only, attempting to clear net man. Players C and D smash any lobs hit short.

12. Over the Net Player *(Intermediates and Advanced—Four Players)*

Two players keep the ball in play hitting only lobs. Two other players are placed near the net on opposite sides. Any lob which goes short is smashed by one of the net players. The player hitting the smash must avoid hitting at the net player opposite him. Score may be kept by counting the number of lobs which clear the players at the net.

13. Serve, Lob, and Cover *(Advanced—Three Players)*

This is a drill for doubles players to practice the serve, the return of serve with a lob, and a third shot which may be a smash or another lob. Here is the sequence of shots: (1) One player serves and moves in to a volleying position; (2) The player returning the serve lobs down the line; the third shot is either an overhead smash by the server's partner at the net or a return lob by the server covering for his partner. The drill stops after three shots. The server should alternate sides, and the players should rotate among positions. A fourth player may be added to the drill as the service returner's partner, and the point may be played out.

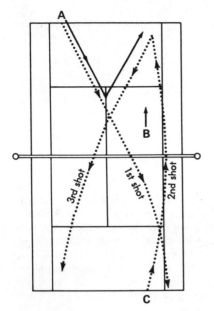

Player A serves, moves to the net and retreats to cover the deep lob.

Player B smashes any short lobs off the return of serve.

Player C returns serve with a lob.

Figure 6-45.

14. Variations (Beginners, Intermediates, and Advanced—Two to Four Players)
There are many variations of the traditional methods of scoring and positioning of players to begin play. Here are some of them which may be used as drills:

1. No Ad Sets. Scoring is conventional, except that when the score reaches deuce, the receiver has the choice of courts and the player who wins the next point wins the game.

2. VASSS Simplified Scoring System. Twenty-one point games; serve changes every five points; players change sides after five, fifteen, and twenty-five points.

3. Tie Breakers. Players practice nine- or twelve-point tie breakers without playing regular games to get used to the pressure created by tie breakers in six-six sets.

4. Two On One. Two players are matched against one; partners defend doubles court, while opponent defends singles court.

5. 15—30 Games. Many coaches feel that the fourth point in a game is the most crucial one; in this variation, play begins with the score at 15—30, and the game is played out from that point.

References

AARON, JAMES E., et al., *First Aid and Emergency Care*. New York: The Macmillan Company, 1972.

ANNARINO, ANTHONY A., *Tennis Individualized Instructional Program*. Englewood Cliffs, N.J.: Prentice-Hall, Inc., 1973.

Athletic Handbook. St. Louis, Mo.: Rawlings Sporting Goods Company, 1971.

BARNABY, JOHN M., *Racket Work: The Key to Tennis*. Boston: Allyn and Bacon, Inc., 1969.

BONNETTE, LOUIS, AND JIM BROWN, "Publicizing a Collegiate Tennis Program," *Tennis Trade* 3, no. 3 (March, 1974), p. 20.

BROWN, JIM, "Coaching Without a Background," *Scholastic Coach* 40, no. 6 (February, 1971), p. 42.

BROWN, JIM, "Do-It-Yourself Tennis Clinic," *The Coaching Clinic* 11, no. 1 (January, 1973), p. 9.

BROWN, JIM, "Flaw Finish: #1, The Service," *Scholastic Coach* 43, no. 9 (May, 1974), p. 44.

BROWN, JIM, "Flaw Finish: #2, The Forehand," *Scholastic Coach* 44, no. 6 (February, 1975), p. 28.

BROWN, JIM, "Flaw Finish: #3, The Backhand," *Scholastic Coach*, 44, no. 7 (March, 1975), p. 8.

BROWN, JIM, "Flaw Finish: #4, The Overhead Smash," *Scholastic Coach* 44, no. 9 (April, 1975), p. 15.

BROWN, JIM, "Flaw Finish: #5, The Volley," *Scholastic Coach* in press.

BROWN, JIM, "How to Go From Doorstop to Dominance in College Tennis," *Tennis Trade* 2, no. 7 (July, 1973), p. 34.

BROWN, JIM, "Newcomers to Tennis Instruction are Often Oldtimers," *Tennis Trade* 2, no. 4 (April, 1973), p. 32.

BROWN, JIM, "Post-Match Scouting in Tennis," *Scholastic Coach* 43, no. 7 (March, 1974), p. 74.

BROWN, JIM, "Psychological Factors in Teaching Tennis to Pre-Teens," *Scholastic Coach* 41, no. 8 (April, 1972), p. 104.

BROWN, JIM, "Recruiting College Tennis Players," *Coach and Athlete* 32, no. 11 (June, 1970), p. 30.

BROWN, JIM, "Seven Cardinal Sins of High School Tennis Players," *Scholastic Coach* 41, no. 7 (March, 1972), p. 68.

BROWN, JIM, "Thinking Lefthanded," *Scholastic Coach* 42 no. 7 (March, 1973), p. 68.

BROWN, JIM, AND BRIAN CHAMBERLAIN, "Anticipation and the Intermediate Tennis Player," *Athletic Journal* 51, no. 9 (May, 1972), p. 38.

EVERETT, PETER, AND VIRGINIA D. SKILLMAN, *Beginning Tennis*. Belmont, Calif.: Wadsworth Publishing Co., Inc., 1968.

GOULD, DICK, *Tennis, Anyone?* (2nd ed.). Palo Alto, Calif.: National Press Books, 1971.

JAEGER, ELOISE M., AND HARRY LEIGHTON, *Teaching of Tennis*. Minneapolis, Minn.: Burgess Publishing Company, 1963.

KENFIELD, JOHN F., JR., *Teaching and Coaching Tennis*. Dubuque, Iowa: Wm. C. Brown Company Publishers, 1964.

SEATON, DON C., et al., *Physical Education Handbook*. Englewood Cliffs, N.J.: Prentice-Hall, Inc., 1969.

UNITED STATES LAWN TENNIS ASSOCIATION, *Official Encyclopedia of Tennis*. New York: Harper and Row, Publishers, Inc., 1972.

WATTENBERG, WILLIAM W., *The Adolescent Years*. New York: Harcourt Brace Jovanovich, Inc., 1973.

Index